Fergie's Finest

Sir Alex Ferguson's First x11

Andrew Kirby

Happy 28th birthday!
From
        Mikey + Meg
            X

ANDREW KIRBY

FERGIE'S FINEST

A White House Publications Book

Published by *White House Publications in 2013*

First print

ANDREW KIRBY

For my dad

ANDREW KIRBY

Who would make *your* 'Team Fergie'?

Ken Loach – Director of 'Looking for Eric'
"Eric Cantona: We don't usually work with stars, but we made an exception for Eric – and what a star! And a team player too. No hair dryer needed on this job!"

Norman Whiteside – ex-Red Hero
"Bryan Robson: without a doubt, the best midfield player of his generation."

Neil Custis – Football writer for* The Sun *newspaper, covering Manchester United and Manchester City.
"Cristiano Ronaldo: For me there has been nobody better that I have witnessed. He was quite simply electric for United."

Scott the Red – Editor of The Republik of Mancunia United fanzine/ blog:
"Ruud Van Nistelrooy: Ruud may not be the most decorated striker at United but his goalscoring record was incredible. Also, he was a bit of a nasty c**t and I like players who have an edge to them."

7

ANDREW KIRBY

CONTENTS

ANDREW KIRBY

Foreword

Sir Alex Ferguson has always loved a good conspiracy theory. Amongst his extra-curricular hobbies – wine appreciation, horseracing – he counts reading books about the assassination of John Fitzgerald Kennedy as one of his most favoured means of 'getting away from it all'.

And, like the death of JFK, Fergie's announcement of his retirement as manager of Manchester United was a real *where were you when* moment.

I was in a car, driving to work. I nearly had to pull over onto the hard shoulder. (Maybe I could have used Sir Alex's patented excuse of "the trots" had the police stopped me.) I felt like turning around, driving home. Calling in sick. I felt as though I'd been punched in the stomach. My mobile phone buzzed with texts. "Is it true?" and "Can you believe it?" they asked.

It caught us all by surprise. It was a short, sharp, shock. And this was a very conscious decision on Sir Alex's part. In 2002 he'd previously announced his retirement months in advance, and he felt the players took their eye off the ball for the rest of the season.

This time, he refused to let anyone lose their focus until the job – winning back the Premier League title from Manchester City – was done.

And sure there'd been whisperings, internet conspiracy theories. The rumour mill had been churning. But when it actually happened, when Fergie brought the curtain down on Wednesday 8th May, thus ending an era, it still left fans, players, and commentators reeling.

When the dust settles, those same observers will testify that the timing was right. Sir Alex is due to undergo a hip operation in summer; David Gill, his main ally on the United board, had already announced *he* was leaving; and United were just about to lift their record twentieth league championship trophy (on Sunday 12th May at Old Trafford, after a match against Swansea City), after seeing off – for the time-being at least, the challenge from the "noisy neighbours" across the city. But on Wednesday 8th May, the feeling was one of exquisite sadness. We hadn't reckoned he would ever leave us, and there were some thought he'd be like his old friend and mentor Jock Stein and be carried off the bench in a

12

coffin…

And indeed, on Wednesday and Thursday, a funereal atmosphere abounded amongst Reds throughout the world. To paraphrase that WH Auden poem, United fans wanted time to stand still, we wanted the clocks stopped, the telephone cut off.

But in reality this was no funeral. Ferguson always hated any comparison between him and "that woman" Margaret Thatcher, and although Fergie's retirement came just weeks after Thatcher's passing, the two were wildly different. Sir Alex Ferguson was to go out with a bang, not a whimper. And as United fans geared up for the mixed emotions of the Sunday game against Swansea, we no longer wanted the pianos silenced, the muffled drum. We came to celebrate. Sir Alex Ferguson has given Manchester United everything, but Fergie has always loved life as much as he loved football, and the time was right, *apt,* for him to go.

We will never see his like again.

He is the most successful manager in the history of English football. His achievements have been legion. But perhaps the greatest of the lot hasn't been the 13 titles in 26 years, nor has it been knocking Liverpool, Arsenal, Chelsea, Manchester City off their respective perches. Nor has it been in building United's own perch so high. No, his major achievement at Manchester United is the million and one happy memories he's given us, and the trophy cabinet full of hopes for the future.

He's given us the permission to dream.

Fergie said: "The decision to retire is one that I have thought a great deal about and one that I have not taken lightly. It is the right time. It was important to me to leave an organisation in the strongest possible shape and I believe I have done so. The quality of this league winning squad, and the balance of ages within it, bodes well for continued success at the highest level whilst the structure of the youth set-up will ensure that the long-term future of the club remains a bright one."

And how.

Ferguson was already considering his legacy on April 22nd, when United wrapped up 'number 20' by beating Aston Villa 3-0 at Old Trafford. When asked after the game for his thoughts on the respective 'greatness' of the 2012-13 United said: "It must bear comparison (with United sides of the past). I'm trying to think of a player who has scored a goal like that (Van Persie's second goal of his hat-trick was described by Fergie as the "goal of the century"). Rafael will end up being compared to Gary Neville. Phil Jones, Rio Ferdinand and Nemanja Vidic are comparable to all the defenders we have had. I'm not saying they are better but great players are great players. Nostalgia does play tricks."

It's not just Sir Alex who's given thought to

'greatest Uniteds'. Fans throughout the world have been talking. On the internet, in the pubs – The Tollgate, Sam Platts, The Trafford – and on the radio. And it's become increasingly clear people *love* to talk about such things. We love our nostalgia. We love to compare and contrast. We love to select our own 'Dream Teams', our 'Fantasy Football x11s'. Sports fans in general love to do this.

In America, baseball fans make studious cases for their team's best ever line-ups. They quote reams of statistics to back up their arguments.

Football, however, is a far more subjective sport. We let our hearts rule our heads. We choose one player over another because of personal feelings, because a certain goal they scored, in maybe a meaningless match, made our heart beat faster, made us love the world, or the game of football again. We choose another player because they might have celebrated a certain goal with the fans, and maybe they high-fived *us* and *us* only, amongst the maelstrom (Ruud Van Nistelrooy high-fived me after a last minute penalty equalizer in Nantes in the Champions League).

But which players deserve to be ranked as the greatest ever in the Ferguson era?

In between Fergie's taking over from Ron Atkinson in 1986 and his retirement in 2013, he handed over 185 players their United debuts. In amongst them we've seen global superstars, and players who've risen up

15

through the United ranks. We've seen big-hearted players who'll give everything for the team, and skilled wizards who are *individually* streets ahead of the rest.

In selecting my 'Team Fergie' for this book I was looking for players who bring the crowd to their collective feet with exhilarating football, or with lion-hearted bravery. I wasn't simply looking for the best players *statistically*. I wasn't merely counting medals or goals scored.

I was looking for the players who've given the fans the fondest memories: the cult heroes; the players who sell the most tee shirts from the stalls outside Old Trafford. The players who've shown us what it means to be a Red. The players who sell the most figurines. The players with the best, and most sung, songs. The players who've downed our rivals.

And in selecting the team, I've canvassed a wide variety of opinions. I've interviewed the editors of fanzines, merchandisers, proud Mancs, and supporters clubs from around the world. I've spoken to ex-players, like Norman Whiteside, and top journalists, like Neil Custis. I've sought out the opinion of Ken Loach, the film director who worked with one Eric Cantona on *Looking for Eric*. I've also interviewed various fans and representatives of rival teams to get a 'view from the enemy': after all, the players they fear, and hate, are likely to be the real United greats.

And what's increasingly become clear is how strongly people *feel* about this, especially in the wake of Sir Alex's retirement as manager. Fans and journalists, fanzine writers and merchandisers alike want to see their own heroes represented.

And thus I've faced a rather complex – but enjoyable – task. It's easier said than done comparing and contrasting the various merits of, say, Denis Irwin and Patrice Evra, or Paul Scholes and Bryan Robson, or Ruud Van Nistelrooy and Wayne Rooney, when you have a pint pot in your hand, when the final decision *doesn't actually matter.*

But here…

Here, I have wavered in the selection of a player for every position. And rightly so. Hell, even Sir Alex himself had difficulties when, in 1997 he selected his own x11 for a club video, and then he'd only been at the club eleven years. Back then he had a paltry 83 players to consider. The blurb for that video suggested Fergie's main selection headaches involved Paul Ince (did he "make the grade?"), David Beckham (did the then "wonder boy" make the cut?), Bryan Robson ("Is Captain Marvel (…) guaranteed selection?") and Brian 'Choccy' McClair (is the player Ferguson "picked most" in the "Ultimate United line up?")

And that's not even considering players like Robin Van Persie, Wayne Rooney, Ruud Van Nistelrooy,

17

Dwight Yorke, Cristiano Ronaldo, Michael Carrick, Jaap Stam, Rio Ferdinand, Nemanja Vidic, and over a hundred others who've arrived at the club *after* 1997.

Phil Martin, Manchester author and match-going Red since 1985, summed up the difficulty I faced in selecting 'Team Fergie': "Sir Alex Ferguson built at least four sides dripping in class so it's a near impossible task to pick his best player for each shirt. It *might* be easier to pick the best team that actually played together. Although how could you separate *that* 1994 team from the 1999-2000 team?"

What *is* clear is that, quite simply, the Ferguson years have been the best time in the world to be a Manchester United fan. During his reign, United won – including Charity/ Community Shields – an eye-watering 38 trophies. And during this time, fans have been lucky enough to have witnessed some of the greatest moments, the greatest players, the greatest teams, in Manchester United's long and proud history.

And *Sir Alex* has been the one common denominator. His drive, his desire, his nature as a winner is now scrawled into the DNA of the club.

This is his legacy.

In my ultimate 'Team Fergie' I have selected, in the main, players which embody this same will to win. Ethel Sleith, the Branch Secretary of the Manchester

United Supporters' Club in South Africa said: "there are players who *wear* the shirt, and there are players who *fit* the shirt."

Only those who truly *fit* the famous Red jersey of Manchester United FC need apply to play in 'Team Fergie'.

I truly hope you enjoy this book, and thanks for reading.

Andrew Kirby

May 2013

1 - Goalkeeper

The last line of defence is our first positional conundrum. There have been some vintage Red 'keepers over the Ferguson years, not least our two Champions League winning custodians, Edwin Van Der Sar and Peter Schmeichel.

Other than those standout performers, United's number ones of Sir Alex's reign fall into three distinct categories: the good, the bad, and the bubbly.

First: the good. Amongst those who might enter the 'good' category are the French World Cup winner Fabien Barthez (although his form was often erratic, and his decision-making often poor), the American, Tim Howard (though his mistake in the Champions League against Jose Mourinho's Porto cost United a place in the quarter-final, and ultimately Howard his place at Old Trafford) and United's current stopper, David De Gea. De Gea is most definitely one for the future. As he gains experience, he is growing into the responsibility that comes with being a United goalie. De Gea's shot-stopping has never been in doubt, but his ability to cope with the more physical aspects of the English game (Andy Carroll) *has* been questioned. De Gea looks to have overcome this now, but as yet he is not the finished goalkeeping article and so we won't consider his claims at length.

Then there's the bad. And make no mistake about it; there were arguably as many goalkeeping disappointments in the Fergie era as there were appalling goalkeeping jerseys. These are the goalkeepers who corked, or a little too vinegary for the taste buds. There's Massimo Taibi, whose blundering performances brought him the brilliant nickname 'The Blind Venetian'. Or Jim Leighton: a man who almost made Saint and Greavesie's tired observations about "Scottish goalkeepers" seem like a prophetic truth – but hell, even a stopped clock is right twice a day. Or Roy Carroll, or Andy Goram. The list could go on.

Finally, there's the bubbly. How about Mark Bosnich, who, having just signed for United, chose to celebrate his wedding night by being locked up in the cells for drunkenness? Hardly an auspicious start to the Aussie's United career: clearly he'd not paid attention to the rumours about his new boss, Sir Alex, and his penchant for hair-dryers.

And then there was Les Sealey. Sealey sadly passed away in 2001, but will be remembered fondly by Reds for his heroics in the FA Cup final replay of 1990, when he was picked ahead of Fergie's customary first-choice, Jim Leighton. In particular, we'll look back on his half-crazed determination (you know what they say about goalkeepers and madness) to stay on the field of play, despite injury. Indeed Les almost punched out the United physio such was his zeal to hang on to the number one jersey now he'd finally gained possession of it.

But, in reality, there are only two serious contenders we can consider for the role of Ferguson's greatest ever United goalkeeper, and we'll examine their respective Red CVs now.

Peter Schmeichel

There used to be a TV ad for Sugar Puffs. It featured the Honey Monster, resplendent in a purple monstrosity of goalkeeping jersey reminiscent of the one worn by United's then 'keeper, Peter Schmeichel. In the ad, the Honey Monster *dwarfed* the goal itself. It looked impossible to score against him because there was simply no eye-of-the-needle space for the ball to thread through. Playing against the *actual* Peter Schmeichel must have felt a lot like that.

United's Great Dane certainly was great. He literally filled the goal. And here I'm not using the word 'literally' in the way that, say, Jamie Redknapp would. I mean it in the non-Sky Sports sense. Schmeichel was a Honey Monster of a goalkeeper: built like a Viking just back from a-rampaging and a-pillaging – maybe he'd had his hair cut for a photo – he was as intimidating as a WWF wrestler who'd just decided to wrestle for real. He could throw the ball further, and with greater accuracy, than most goalkeepers could kick it, and indeed, when a rogue fan invaded the pitch in a Champions League clash with Galatasaray at Old Trafford Schmeichel launched *him* off the pitch too. This throw must hold some kind of Guinness World Record: perhaps the furthest human shot-put pitch.

On the continent, there are a series of jokes which most Europeans find inexplicably funny. Perhaps there's been something lost in translation. The gist of them is that Chuck Norris is super-tough: the epitome of masculinity. Here's one: "Chuck Norris can kill two stones with one bird." Well, you can quite easily play a similar game with Schmeichel. How about this one: Schmeichel's hands were so big, he could hold a size 5 football in his palm like it was a marble. Or: When Bruce Banner gets mad he turns into the Hulk. When the Hulk gets mad he turns into Peter Schmeichel. When Peter Schmeichel gets mad, run.

Schmeichel terrified opposing strikers. He was the master of the one-on-one situation: his impromptu 'star jumps' as he came out to confront an approaching attacker often left them as quivering wrecks on the Old Trafford turf. He yelled at his defenders louder than the noisiest crowd. He made miraculous saves and he made them look easy, as though he'd made them for the cameras. Often he made saves you couldn't imagine any other keeper making *one handed,* and he'd hold on to the ball too like the palms of his gloves had been daubed with superglue.

Signed for a cut-price £560,000 from Brondby - Fergie dubbed the deal "the bargain of the century" - Peter Schmeichel was, throughout the 1990s, undoubtedly the world's best goalkeeper. Not only did this colossus, who reputedly had to have his triple-XL shirts tailor-made for him, play a major part in helping unfashionable Denmark win the 1992 European Championships, he also formed the bedrock of the Manchester United team which conquered all before them domestically during the decade, and was in goal when we finally won back the European Cup, in its new guise as the Champions League, in 1999, a full 31 years after the first time we'd got our hands on the trophy.

Though he initially struggled with some aspects of the English game – particularly crosses: his aversion to them calling some to dub him 'Dracula' – it was soon clear Schmeichel was a serious goalkeeper. In his first season for the Reds, Schmeichel and co came heartbreakingly close to winning the league championship, but were eventually pipped to the post by cross-Pennine rivals, Leeds United. The Red Devils had led the way by six points at the end of September, and though the gap was closed to a single point by the end of March, United fans still believed a first top division title in a quarter of a century *could* be on the horizon. The case for United's defence, so often United's weak-point during the seventies and eighties when they were an exciting cup team, but no great shakes in the league, was being eloquently stated by players like Denis Irwin and Gary Pallister, and practically yelled by Peter Schmeichel, the Great Dane who was already our undisputed number 1.

Indeed, United's defence remained mean all season. No: what derailed our championship challenge of 1991-92 was the fact the goals dried up. April truly was the cruellest month for United. It saw a series of disappointing draws which earlier in the season would have been converted into wins. Then, even more damagingly, United lost at home to Nottingham Forest (2-1) and then away at West Ham's Upton Park, that perennial graveyard of Red dreams. Leeds went on to wrap up the title on 2nd May, by narrowly beating Norwich at home by a single goal to nil. And though United put Tottenham Hotspur to the sword – 3-1 – on the same day, it was not enough.

There was something of an end of an era feel to that final day of the season. Not only was it the last day of the English First Division – next year, the brand-spanking new, all-singing, all-dancing Premier League would begin – but it was the final hurrah for standing in the Stretford End. In 1992-93, the famous terrace would be replaced by an all-seater stand, in the wake of the Taylor Report. But there were also renewed hopes for the future. United had, finally, found a rock-like defence, and, with some fresh impetus further up the field, perhaps they'd finally lay that twenty-six year curse to rest, and win the league.

Peter Schmeichel's confidence – never exactly fragile even in the worst of times – was given a boost over the summer of 1992 as he led unfancied Denmark to a famous European Championships triumph. He returned to Old Trafford as a bonafide leader. Soon it would emerge that United had leaders all over the park that season, but in Schmeichel, they had that all-important foundation. The Great Dane kept an astounding twenty-two clean sheets in 1992-93 as United finally killed the albatross which had been around their necks since 1967.

And once we'd won one, we just couldn't stop. In 1993-94, with the shackles removed, the Reds romped to the Premier League title in rare style. United's defensive record during this period was miserly. Centre-halves Steve Bruce and Gary Pallister played out of their skins simply to avoid a rollicking from the big goalkeeper who was breathing down their necks.

Schmikes was also an inspiration going forward too. As we've mentioned, his fearsome throws set up countless Red attacks. And he even took to lumbering forward into the opposition box himself in *hail Mary* Fergie time if United were desperate for a goal. His presence created havoc amongst opposition defenders, and freed up space for our best headers of the ball to have a run on goal. Hell, he was a dangerous attacker in his own right: in a 1995 UEFA Cup match against Rotor Volgograd at Old Trafford, Schmeichel scored a *half-volley* to level the scores late, late on, however United couldn't grab the required second goal and were knocked out on away goals.

A commentator's cry of: "And the big goalkeeper's coming up" for a late corner as United chased games down became a familiar refrain. Most famously, this occurred in the 1999 Champions League final against Bayern Munich in Barcelona. As the game ticked into injury time, United won a corner. Desperate to find a goal to level the game after Bayern had held an early lead throughout most of the match, Schmeichel, who was United's captain for the night because of Roy Keane's suspension, was seen gesturing wildly to the United bench. And, after a nod from Fergie, the Great Dane charged forward and into the box.

David Beckham took the corner and, with Schmeichel occupying two Bayern defenders who might otherwise have been marking Sheringham and Yorke, the ball broke loose. After some frenzied pinball, Giggs attempted a shot, but miscued. Fortunately it fell to Sheringham, who guided the ball into the corner of the net.

Cue frenzy.

Schmeichel didn't go up for United's second corner in the three minutes' injury time which had been allocated. But by then the damage had been done. And after Solksjaer won it for Manchester United, it was Peter Schmeichel, pictured on TV cameras across the world cart-wheeling with unbridled joy, who was one of the happiest men in the stadium. United had won the Treble.

We talked of the ends of eras earlier. And indeed, mixed up in all of the melting pot of emotions on that wonderful night in Barcelona, there was some sadness. For Schmeichel, we already knew, had played his last game for the club. He was moving on to pastures new: Sporting Lisbon of Portugal would provide him with a less highly pressurised environment in which he could see out the rest of his career.

No United player in the history of this famous club has ever left on such a high note. Only Fergie himself, when lifting the Premier League title at Old Trafford in his final home match as manager of the club comes close.

There's one small afterword on Schmeichel, however. It seemed life in the Portuguese league just didn't cut it for a man so used to the cut and thrust of the Premier League. And it wasn't long before we saw him again, this time in the Aston Villa number 1 shirt. That felt really wrong, like seeing internet photos of a former girlfriend with her new *beau*. Worse was to come. Schmeichel signed for Manchester rivals City, in a move some Reds saw as unforgivable. At City, Schmeichel even had the audacity to perform a "blue cart-wheel" after *they* scored against us, as was noted by the Manchester author Phil Martin.

And yet, whenever we look back on footage of those 'star jump' saves in one-on-ones, whenever we see the stills of that stunning one-handed catch, whenever we recall *that* penalty save from Bergkamp in the 1999 FA Cup semi-final against Arsenal at Villa Park, or hear that famous line of punditry from ex-Red boss Ron Atkinson - "the big goalie's coming up" – we can't help but feel the hairs on the backs of our necks standing on end. Schmeichel played close to four hundred competitive games for United, and in every one he did something unorthodox, something special which made him the one of a select breed of United greats we'll never forget.

Edwin Van Der Sar

Replacing Schmeichel was no mean feat. As we'll see later, particularly in our piece on Roy Keane, replacing a Red legend is often an arduous task. Not many could fill the Great Dane's famous triple-XL shirt. Though many tried - as we saw in our introduction - none, it seemed, had the stature, the commanding presence, of the Great Dane. Big, tall, World Cup-winners, Americans, Italians, Australians. Big money buys and those with big reputations. All tried, all failed.

Until the anti-Peter Schmeichel came along and stole our Red hearts. Tall, but reedy-thin and staggeringly laid back, Edwin Van Der Sar was about as far from Schmeichel as it was possible to be: he looked like a high school chess champion stretched on a rack (or perhaps he'd been sat on by Schmikes). The Dutchman was flat as one of the pancakes used to be served up in the Dutch Pancake House in St. Peter's Square, but in his claiming the number 1 jersey, and *fitting* it…

Well, there was something very 'Sword in the Stone' about it all.

Certainly, along with Schmeichel, Van Der Sar was one of only two goalkeepers who've been between the sticks when the Holy Grail was delivered during the Fergie era: the Dutchman kept goal for the Champions League final in 2008, in Moscow, when his penalty heroics - ably assisted by John Terry's slip - helped secure a third European Cup for the reds. And it was his save, from Nicolas Anelka's sudden death spot-kick, which finally saw red ribbons being hung from the famous trophy.

Edwin, our star, joined United an undisclosed fee, believed to be around £2 million, in June 2005. Undoubtedly, this was another "bargain of the century" for Ferguson, as the Holland international went on to play 266 competitive matches for the Reds, and helped deliver four Premier League titles, one Champions League, and two League Cups.

And though Van Der Sar came to United with some question marks over his head – was he already too old? Was he commanding enough? – we shouldn't have doubted him for a minute. In fact, Van Der Sar had already enjoyed a very successful career when he joined the Reds, having represented the European heavyweights Ajax and Juventus (he played for both in Champions League finals), and having garnered a wealth of Premier League experience, having played for Fulham for four years. And United had already shown an interest in signing the Dutchman four years earlier, after Edwin lost his place in the Juventus team to a young (and ultra-expensive) Gianluigi Buffon. But Fulham had got in there first and it was left to United fans to consider what might have been.

Van Der Sar radiated calm. His presence seemed to allow the United defence to relax, get on with their games with the minimum of fuss. United were trailing in Chelsea's slipstream when he joined – thanks primarily to Abramovich's billions – and for the first couple of seasons, but in 2007, Van Der Sar helped the Reds reclaim "our trophy". And again, it was his ability when faced with a penalty which proved crucial. In early May, he saved a Manchester City spot-kick which meant United went on to win the derby 1-0. Twenty-four hours later, Chelsea had to win against Arsenal – at Arsenal – to maintain any hope of retaining their Premier League crown. They didn't, and United had their trophy back.

Van Der Sar's prowess when facing penalties was again on show in the traditional curtain-raiser to the new season, the Community Shield, in which he kept out three Chelsea penalties on the trot as United marched on to win the shield. 2007-08 was easily Van Der Sar's best in a United shirt, and it was fitting that it was bookended, with his shoot-out heroics, in both occasions against Chelsea, in the Champions League final in Moscow.

Moscow was the first of three Champions League finals Van Der Sar played for the Reds. He also played twice against Barcelona, in Rome and at Wembley, though he could do nothing about United's defeats on these occasions. In the 2011 final, the Dutchman became the second oldest player to appear in a Champions League final. He was well over 40 years old by this point and the Barcelona defeat was to be his last game before retirement. Unfortunately, he couldn't go out on a high like Schmeichel, but he did rack up an impressive trophy haul with the Reds.

He also set some outstanding records. In 2009, for example, he kept an incredible *eleven* consecutive clean sheets – that's 1,311 minutes without being beaten – which was a world record for a top-flight 'keeper. In total, he kept 21 clean sheets that season, allowing United to beat arch-rivals Liverpool to the title.

The Dutchman was also extremely popular with fans. In 2010 when there was talk of Edwin retiring, fans consistently chanted their desire for him to stay. And it worked: he signed a new one-year contract which would take him up to the end of the 2011 season. That year, the songs demanding that he stayed started even earlier, around Christmas time, however this time, Edwin wasn't for turning. He'd had an extremely long innings as a 'keeper, however, and probably deserved to finally put those long legs, and big feet, up for a while.

Verdict: Though Van Der Sar played in three Champions League finals to Schmeichel's one, they both finished their careers with the Reds with one Champions League medal to their names. And Schmeichel's Champions League triumph came *as captain,* and secured United's unique treble.

And though Van Der Sar was very popular amongst match-going Reds – witness those chants for him to stay – Schmeichel was possibly the most popular goalkeeper United have ever had. Scott the Red, editor of the excellent United blog-site 'The Republik of Mancunia' agrees: "I'd have Schmeichel as goalie, just…"

That *just* probably comes from the fact the Great Dane blotted his Red copybook ever so slightly by joining Manchester City. Otherwise he'd be a far more resounding choice. Phil Martin agrees: "No disrespect to Edwin but Schmeichel is a certainty, despite the blue cartwheel…"

2 - Right Full-Back

United's right-backs have, over the Ferguson years, been a rather buccaneering bunch. Often, they have proved as eager to get forward as they are to defend. They start attacks, or else maintain the pressure on the opposition as United steam forward. They work in devastating tandem with the right-winger who is (nominally) playing in front of them, and make over-lapping runs, creating vital space. United right full-backs are told to stand on the post when the Reds are defending corners, but they can just as likely be found winning corners of our own.

There are three stand-out performers to consider for this role. The current incumbent, Rafael Da Silva, the arch-Red Gary Neville, and Paul Parker, who played the role when United finally won the league title again, after that agonising twenty-six year wait.

Rafael Da Silva

If not for the efforts of Robin Van Persie and his one-in-a-million strikes against Aston Villa (as United reclaimed the Premier League crown from Manchester City in 2012-13) and Wigan Athletic (his first goal for the Reds), Rafael Da Silva might have had a clean-sweep when it came to United's goals of the 2012-13 season.

First there was his miracle goal at Anfield, which dragged United back into a game they'd been fading badly in (United went on to win 2-1, with RVP slotting home the winner from the spot). And then there was his bolt from the blue against Harry Redknapp's Queens Park Rangers at Loftus Road, a devastating shot of such venom that had 'keeper (and fellow Brazilian) Julio Cesar got his hand to it, would have probably broken every bone. The celebrations following this wonder goal – Rio Ferdinand jabbing a finger at Rafael as though to say *you da man* – showed just how good Rafa's United teammates thought the goal was.

What's more, you could see Redknapp shaking his head in that hangdog way of his, as though to say *and that strike was by their right-back? How can we compete with that?*

It certainly was a strike of unique quality from Rafa. But our right-back is not exactly unique himself. He comes as a part of a matching pair, with his identical twin brother Fabio (who, as fate would have it was actually on loan at QPR when United faced them, though under the terms of the loan agreement he wasn't allowed to play). Indeed, so alike are the two that, without the names on the backs of their shirts, even their Red teammates might not be able to tell them apart. And this striking similarity between the two led to all kinds of rumours of high jinks. Even with Fabio in London and Rafael in Manchester, Rafael was pictured in one game wearing boots with his twin's name stitched into them, giving rise to some suggestions they might have pulled the wool over everyone's eyes and performed a swap.

And in October 2009, Fabio was even booked for a foul committed by his twin.

An easy mistake to make.

Rafael and his twin are slightly built. But they are deceptively strong. And brave. They both have a mop of curly black hair. They're quick. The archetypal buccaneering United right full-backs. And after United's experiences with not so 'brazilliant' Brazilians (Kleberson immediately springs to mind) Rafael in particular has been like a breath of fresh air. More recently, Rafa has also shown signs he's lost some of that hot-headedness which defined his early career, and which proved so costly, such as in his sending off against Bayern Munich in the Champions League quarter final of 2010, when United ultimately lost a game they'd dominated.

Rafael Pereira da Silva was born in the sun-kissed state of Rio de Janeiro. He moved to the rainy city of Manchester in 2008, along with his twin, but they'd been on the United radar for some time before that. It was Red scout Les Kershaw who first spotted them, playing for Fluminense in a tournament in Hong Kong in 2005. Kershaw described the pair as "two little whippets", and there's still a dogged, determined quality to them both now.

They were still only 17 when they joined United, and it must have taken some guts for them to leave behind everything they knew to come and join the biggest club in the world. But they certainly didn't show they were in any way cowed. They took everything in their stride, almost from the off, and so impressed the United staff that they were soon incorporated into the first team squad. Rafael was the first to make his debut – as a substitute in the inaugural match of the 2008-09 Premier League season against Newcastle. A month later, he started in the League Cup, that traditional finishing school for young United starlets, but also in the Champions League, away at Danish side Aalborg. And again, he showed no fear.

He soon became something of a regular pick for Fergie, and his form went from strength to strength. Indeed, by the end of the season, the standard of his performances was recognised as he was nominated for the PFA Young Player of the Year award (although Ashley Young, then of Aston Villa, won the honour). The season had also seen Rafael's first goal for the Reds: a blockbuster against Arsenal which was nearly as good as his QPR strike in 2013.

And though his form dipped somewhat in the following season, his United career has continued on its upward trajectory. Stuart Matheson, the *Manchester Evening News'* United reporter characterised the Brazilian's transformation as from "impetuous to imperious". Now, at twenty-two, Rafa is United's undisputed first-choice right full-back. In 2012, he was rewarded for his form by an 'upgrade' of his shirt number: he's now moved up from '21' to '2': Gary Neville's old shirt number. And the Brazilian Gary Neville (is Fabio the Brazilian Phil?) now has three Premier League winner's medals, one League Cup winner's medal, and one Club World Cup winner's medal in his own personal trophy cabinet. Hopefully, given his tender age, there'll be plenty more to come.

Gary Neville

If Rafael Da Silva is the Brazilian Gary Neville, what about the *original* Gary Neville?

There's something about watching a home-grown player making it in the first team. Fans feel a real sense of paternal pride about it. Joy too. And there's a sense that supporters are willing to forgive a home-grown player *just that little bit more* than a player they've imported from another club, or country. We love them because we can see just how much it means to them to play for the club they've grown up as a part of. And we love them just that little bit more if they show the same desire, the same determination, the same commitment we sneakily hope *we'd* bring to the United cause if we ever got called to lace up our boots. And, more than that, we love them when they love United. We're not talking kissing the badge after scoring a goal here. Anybody can do that. And they're just as likely to put in a transfer request the next week. No, we're talking an absolute, all-encompassing passion for the Reds which the players in question simply cannot hide.

These types of players don't need to kiss the badge. The badge is already tattooed onto their very souls.

Gary Neville is that type of player. Red Nev is, according to Phil Martin, "a true red legend who moved up through every rank imaginable and made right back his own". He celebrated United goals – the vast majority of which hadn't been scored by him - as though he was a fan on the pitch. This was particularly the case when United were playing against Liverpool. Yeah, Red Nev loved it when we scored against Liverpool.

As the song so succinctly put it: "Gary Neville is a Red; he hates Scousers."

The loathing was, of course, mutual. The very best you could say about Red Nev was that he "divided opinion as a player". And it shows what a good job he's now doing as a pundit on Sky Sports that everyone is, for once, agreed that he's great. Neville, it is clear, has a wealth of knowledge about the game he loves. He's opinionated, and, a rarity amongst pundits, he's not scared of stating his opinion. He's also surprisingly articulate, "literally" putting people like Jamie "Literally" Redknapp to shame. It is clear Neville puts the work in, does his research.

But then Red Nev has always worked hard. He talks of how he started in the United youth team as a Centre Back, and how every year as they culled the youngsters it was thought wouldn't make it at Old Trafford, he was sure he'd be one of them. And so, he trained extra hard. Put the hours in at the gym and on the training pitches. Swotted up on tactics, on the opposition, on ways to make himself a better player. And stayed. His brother, Phil – now at Everton - was always regarded as the better prospect of the two, but it was Gary who eventually stayed the distance at United, pulling on the famous Red shirt a total of 602 times, and becoming, as Phil Martin says "a true Red legend".

In Jaap Stam's infamous book, *Head to Head* (the contents of which are thought to have led to his untimely exit from the club) he described Gary and Phil Neville as "busy little c**ts". The big Dutchman actually meant this affectionately. And "busy" would be a good description of Gary Neville's United career. He was "busy" winning trophies, "busy" making the right full-back berth his own, "busy" endearing himself to United fans. The son of (the wonderfully named) Neville Neville became like a son to us all. And if there wasn't widespread tears on the announcement of his retirement in 2011 – as there was when Eric Cantona, say, announced *his* – this was because Neville, and United fans knew he'd called time on his distinguished career *at the right time.* Before he was in danger of tarnishing his reputation.

Red Nev's final game in a Red shirt came at The Hawthorns, in a Premier League clash against West Brom. The match was an early kick-off on

New Year's Day, 2011, and that day Gary Neville played as though he was as hungover as most of the fans. He'd clearly lost his pace and could have given away at least three penalties. He eventually announced his retirement a month later, but he's since said that he *knew* that game would be his last for the club. He'd become a liability to the side he loved.

And oh how he loved it. And oh how that love blossomed. In his time at Old Trafford, Red Nev won an incredible eight Premier League winner's medals (and it is only because miracle man Ryan Giggs has won *thirteen* that we're not blown away by this). He also won a Champions League, three FA Cups, two League Cups, a Club World Cup, two Turtle Doves and a Partridge in a Pear Tree.

Red Nev was, after Ryan Giggs, the first of the new wave of youth team stars who burst onto the first-team scene in the 1990s. He made his United debut in a UEFA Cup clash with Torpedo Moscow in 1992, and though his first-team appearances were initially limited by the presence of the England international, Paul Parker, by 1995, he'd become a fixture in the side. His right-flank

47

partnership with fellow youth team graduate and great friend David Beckham (Red Nev was Best Man at Becks' wedding) was to become one of the key aspects of United's developing side during this period, and Neville's over-lapping runs, and his often underestimated quality when crossing the ball, helped contribute to a great number of United goals, though Neville rarely troubled the scoreboard himself.

Perhaps Neville's proudest moments in a United shirt, however, came when he was made Club Captain upon Roy Keane's departure in 2005. Never has a United captain been more suitably selected. Supporters got the impression he'd die for the club if he had to. Certainly he'd bleed for it.

"O Captain! My Captain!"

Paul Parker

Paul Parker was the man whose place Gary Neville eventually took in the United first-team. Parker signed for United in August 1991, moving from

QPR for a fee of £2 million. And though this was seen as rather an exorbitant sum, at the time, Parker was the England right-back. He'd starred for the national side in the 1990 World Cup in Italy, when they nearly went all the way to the final. Unfortunately for Paul though, it was his back upon which a West German shot was deflected for the opening goal in that semi-final in Turin. This unfortunate deflection notwithstanding, it was clear that in Parker United were buying *quality*. They were also buying the blueprint right full-back for the Ferguson era: a right-back who was quick and comfortable on the ball, who could drive forward and find space, who could cross it (Parker made up for the deflected goal against the West Germans by crossing for Lineker to turn home in the World Cup semi-final).

Paul Parker was an integral part of the team which won United's first league title for over a quarter of a century in 1993. His pace and his ability were crucial to the way that side played: he was almost a 'wing-back', driving the team forward and forming useful partnerships with both Andrei Kanchelskis and Lee Sharpe. Helping United to blossom into the free-scoring unit they were to become.

Injury, however, was to blight Parker's later career with the Reds. And eventually when the young buck Gary Neville came along, he lost his place in the side. He scored two United goals in almost 150 games for the club. One of those came in a stunning 4-1 home win to Spurs which was a 'statement of intent' match as United plotted a course to that vital first Premier League win. In addition to *that* title, he was to win one more Premier League, as well as an FA Cup and a League Cup.

Verdict: Gary Neville is the obvious choice. Indeed, Red Nev has such a strong claim for a place in the side he could even be considered for the captaincy. He was tough and hardworking, bled for the cause and put in tackle after tackle.

But he was also in possession of more skill than he was given credit for. David Beckham notwithstanding, Gary Neville was often the best crosser of the ball at the club.

Red Nev's sheer trophy haul, his legendary appearance stats, and his overweening passion for the club make him by far the greatest right-back to have played for United during Ferguson's tenure. Though Rafael has time on his side, he'd need to go some way to replace this particular "busy c**t".

3 - Centre Half

You want your centre half to run through brick walls for your team. You want them to *look* like a brick wall to the opposition forwards. You want them to be ramparts, fortifications, barricades. You want to be able to describe them using the following adjectives: unyielding, unbreakable, durable, hard-as-nails. You want them to be *stalwarts*. You want them no-nonsense, tackle-first-ask-questions-later.

Some very hard men have played centre-half for United under Alex Ferguson, and, if you dare, lets take a look at some of the greatest of these big, bad, b******s.

Jaap Stam

Picture the scene. It's 2012-13, and United are already three to the good away from home. They're cruising: the match is won. The fans are cruising too, and they're in full voice. Only, instead of singing about the current goal-scoring hero, they're waxing lyrical about a centre-half who left the club under something of a cloud early in the 2001-02 season.

United fans are prone to digging out the back catalogue in terms of singing about players, but, after songs in homage to King Eric Cantona, there's only one player who's as popular in the United fans' repertoire. And that's Jaap Stam: the uncompromising, yet surprisingly skilful Dutch centre half, who played only three seasons for United, but who's remained in fans' hearts for much, much longer.

The song isn't brilliant, lyrically. But it isn't half catchy: "Yip Jaap Stam is a big Dutch man, get past him if you f***ing can, try a little trick and he'll make you look a d**k, Yip Jaap, Jaap Stam."

There's another reason Stam still gets mentioned today in dispatches from Old Trafford. And that's because, famously, Fergie calls Stam his one big regret. Over the years, Sir Alex proved himself to be adept at 'letting players go' at the right times in their career. Apparently he saw something in their eyes; a slight slackening in their drive, their hunger. And in most of these cases, he was proved correct: think Hughes, Ince, Ruud Van Nistelrooy, Beckham maybe. But Stam, Fergie admits, he let go too soon. And sure there was a big bid from Lazio which was supposedly too good to turn down. And sure, Stam hadn't helped himself with some ill-advised comments in his book – *Head to Head* - about Fergie 'tapping him up' prior to his transfer from PSV Eindhoven (Stam joined for £10.6 million in 1998). But still, Yip Jaap had another seven seasons at the top level in Italy and Holland (where he represented Lazio, Milan and Ajax) before he hung up his boots.

Jaap Stam was built like The Thing in the American comic, *The Fantastic Four*. He looked as though he'd been hewn from rock. His head was a hunk of stone. He had absolutely no fear and, as the song goes, if any forward tried a little trick, he did indeed make them look "a d**k". He only ever scored one goal for United, in a 6-2 victory at Leicester, but that didn't matter, because Jaap, you *knew*, didn't care about all of that. Jaap Stam cared about one thing and one thing only, and that was defending.

Stam was a great defender: tough in the tackle and quick over short distances, *always* positionally aware and good on the ball. He seemed to combine the best in continental defending with stubborn, English grit. In his time at Old Trafford, he was an undoubted *winner*. He won medal after medal, including the Big Three, the treble, in one amazing season in 1999. (He also won two further Premier League titles, and an Intercontinental Cup.)

1999 was undoubtedly his best season at United. That year, he was simply a level above most of the other central defenders in the Premier League, and he was an absolute beast in European competition too. United's team at the time was possibly the strongest we've ever had, both mentally and physically. They never knew they were beaten. And the *spine* of that side – Schmeichel, Stam, Keane – was fearsome. That trio allowed the rest of the team to play. They were the bedrock upon which the trickery of the Cole and Yorke duo flourished, and through which the astounding wing-play of Beckham and Giggs was given the space to perform.

All together now: "Yip Jaap Stam is a big Dutch man…"

Nemanja Vidic

Speaking of defenders with popular songs in their honour, the undoubted current favourite is Nemanja Vidic. His particular ditty, which will surely stand the test of time even when Vidic's many injuries finally take their toll and he leaves the club, goes like this: "Nemanja, wo-oh-oh-oh, Nemanja wo-oh-oh-oh, He comes from Serbia, he'll f***ing murder ya." Which is something of an exaggeration, but does have its *basis* in the truth.

Vidic is the closest United have come to Jaap Stam since the big Dutchman left in 2001-02. The Serb also scores highly on the cult-hero stakes. According to Phil Bedford from T-Shirts United Vidic is one of the few heroes from today's United team whose shirts sell at anywhere near the levels of previous Fergie favourites like Cantona, Stam, and Solksjaer – and he is certainly the only defender.

And though he doesn't *look* like a brick wall like Stam did – indeed, if you've ever seen Vidic up close and in person, you're actually taken aback by how *normal-sized* he is – any opposition player who's ever had the pleasure of crashing into him will know the sheer power contained within him. It is as though his skeleton has been constructed of some incredibly heavy metal, like tungsten. If you've ever studied your chemistry, you'll know that tungsten comes from the Swedish for "heavy stone". And you'll also know that it has some toxic qualities.

Nemanja Vidic too: he's poison to opposing forwards.

Vidic signed for United for £7 million in the January transfer-window of 2006 from Spartak Moscow, having begun his career at Red Star Belgrade. He'd come to prominence as a key member of the Serbian national team's "Famous Four" defenders who would concede just a single goal during their qualification campaign for the 2006 World Cup. He made his Red debut as a substitute for Ruud Van Nistelrooy in the League Cup semi-final against Blackburn, and later that season, the League Cup was to become the first trophy he won in United colours when the Reds beat Wigan Athletic 4-0 in the final in Cardiff (Vidic had again been substitute in the final).

During the next season, however, United's number 15 became the definite first-choice centre-half, alongside Rio Ferdinand. This chalk-and-cheese partnership was to become one of the finest in the Premier League for many seasons. They were to win the league title four times over the next five years and five out of the next seven, and, after Gary Neville's departure, Vidic was to captain the side for much of this period. Individually, his performances were also recognised. In 2008-09, he was nominated for the PFA Player of the Year award (although Ryan Giggs later won it), and was given the double honour of being named United fans, and players, player of the year. And in 2010, Vida had the pleasure of scoring the thousandth goal at Old Trafford in the Premier League era.

It wasn't all glory for the Serb, however. He suffered his fair share of disciplinary trouble, particularly against Liverpool. He struggled against the pace of their then star-forward Fernando Torres, and often let the red-mist descend. He was sent-off against United's bitter Merseyside rivals in October 2009 (in a 2-0 defeat), and September 2010 (in a 3–2 triumph). He also saw red in other big games. In 2011, he was sent-off against Chelsea late on in a game the London club went on to win 2-1. However, the Serb was to attain vengeance in May of that year when his goal helped United to a 2-1 win against the Stamford Bridge club, and virtually secure the title for the Reds (they eventually went on to win the title against Blackburn a week later). Revenge against Liverpool would take a little longer. But in January 2013, it finally came: Vidic deflecting in an Evra header at Old Trafford to consign the Anfield club to a 2-1 defeat as United continued their procession to a record twentieth Premier League title.

But first, Vidic had to suffer a spell of debilitating injuries. His 2011-12 season was ruined. First by a calf problem, then by a knee injury suffered against Basel in the Champions League. The second injury was far more serious: Vidic was stretchered off and would miss the remainder of the season. And without his might and strength at the back, United lost out on the championship on goal difference to Manchester City. He was missed badly.

He returned, of course, and in some style, as United fought tooth-and-nail to reclaim their crown. Ferguson was managing his fitness levels now though, and Vidic rarely played more than one game a week. Still, he played against the big boys, and his renewal of that age-old partnership with Rio, allied with the fact that this time it was City who lost a key centre-half (Kompany) for a chunk of the season, ensured United won the title with four games to spare.

Vidic, you can be sure, will still be sung about *long, long* after he finally hangs up his boots. He's put his body on the line for the Red cause for seven highly successful years now, and it is starting to take its toll. He's loved by the fans and players alike, and he's taken his fair share of broken noses, knackered knees, and strained calves. But for now he remains the archetypal United captain, and a bonafide Red hero.

Steve Bruce

Steve Bruce is the one United man who could out-broken-nose Nemanja Vidic. The big Geordie's war-wounds were written all over his face, as was his inclination to bravely stick his face in, even though he might have it kicked off.

There have been some famous noses at Old Trafford, not least Fergie's own reddish-tinged beak, but Steve Bruce's has to be the most distinctive of them all. By the end of his career, it looked as though someone had been at it with a potato-masher. It was squashed, zigzagged, stewed across his face. It was said that Sir Alex had promised to grant Bruce not just a testimonial but a nose-job upon the United number 4's completion of 10 years at the club.

But Brucie wasn't only famed for his nose. He was also the man responsible for the original "Fergie Time" goals. It was April 1993 and United were in the shake-up to be the first team to win the inaugural Premier League. But thoughts of the previous season's slump as we came close to the finishing line, and of how Howard Wilkinson's Leeds United had pipped the Reds right at the last, still haunted United fans. Then, a cruel April had proved Manchester United's downfall, and, when Sheffield Wednesday took a second-half lead through a John Sheridan penalty it looked as though it might be a case of history repeating itself.

United huffed and puffed, desperately trying to find a way back into the match, but Sheffield

Wednesday, a team with their tails-up – they'd recently reached their first FA Cup final after defeating city rivals United in a Wembley semi-final – held firm. Time was slipping through the hourglass far more quickly than either fans or players would have liked, but thankfully, there'd be a decent amount of injury time after the referee, Michael Peck, was injured and had to be replaced by one of the linesmen, John Hilditch, on the hour. And this is what's often forgotten, lost in the hysteria and outrage: the seven added minutes in the game were completely justified.

But the myth always makes for more interesting reading than the reality, and the myth says that United are always given more time to score – more Fergie Time – than any other team.

So be it. But unlike other teams, United plug away to the last and, even when Steve Bruce popped up with a wondrous 85th minute equalizer, from a Denis Irwin corner, the Reds *kept going*. Looking for an unlikely winner (as would be echoed in Barcelona in 1999, and at Old Trafford, against Liverpool, in 1999, and on countless other occasions). The first goal, Bruce's equalizer, had been his first goal in a United shirt since October, which was actually quite a drought in Brucie terms; for a centre-half he was something of a prolific scorer. And it brought a groundswell of relief throughout the stadium. The second, Bruce's fairytale winner, cued euphoric scenes: Kiddo on his knees on the pitch; Fergie trying out his now famous granddad jig. And in the crowd, pandemonium.

Glorious, thankful pandemonium.

Further Brucie bonuses came in Europe. Famously, Steve Bruce never represented the national team. This was not necessarily a bad thing, given the sheer number of times Bryan Robson returned from England duty injured, given how Beckham and Rooney would become the nation's favourite villains, and given how Paul Scholes was so woefully misused - like having a Ferrari, but preferring to use it to tow a caravan. So United's run in the European Cup Winners' Cup in the 1990-91 season became like Bruce's very own international tournament. He rose to the occasion on famous European nights at Old Trafford, and played out of his skin on foreign fields across the continent. More lion-hearted than any other English defender of his era, he also brought with him a useful eye for a goal. Over the course of that vintage year for Bruce, which culminated in the Cup Winners' Cup win in Rotterdam against Barcelona, he scored an incredible nineteen times in all competitions. And although some were penalties, he weighed in with more than his fair share of bullet-headers.

It was astounding how far the Geordie had come since his first division debut (in 1984 for Norwich, after a successful early spell at Gillingham) in which he scored an own goal in the very first minute, against Liverpool. But then, he'd always had an irrepressible fighting spirit. Though Norwich were relegated in his first season, they also won the League Cup (Bruce was voted man of the match in the final) and he stayed for the following season to help the Norfolk side to yoyo straight back up again. And by 1987, he was starting to attract the attention of the big boys. United eventually won the race for his signature, beating off strong competition from Tottenham Hotspur and Glasgow Rangers, for a fee of around £800,000.

Despite playing well for the Reds during his first couple of seasons, it was with the arrival of his defensive partner in crime Gary Pallister in 1989 that Steve Bruce really came into his own. Bruce and Pallister went together like Starsky and Hutch, like chips and gravy, like long-lost brothers from the north east of England. They were on the same wavelength. They enjoyed defending together. They enjoyed dragging United up from the doldrums, steadying the ship, and then putting them on course for, first an FA Cup win in 1990, then the European Cup Winners' Cup in 1991, then the League Cup in 1992, and then finally, in 1993, they delivered the long lusted-after league title for the Reds.

The following season, with the shackles off, United were far and away the best team in the land. With Brucie as captain, United saw off all-comers to win the league and FA Cup double for the first time in the club's history. Interestingly, Bruce was the first English captain to pull off this feat for any club in the twentieth century. But in 1994-95, United couldn't muster the same energy. They didn't dominate the season and win with panache as they had in 1993-94, with that dream team that simply dripped off the tongue: Schmeichel - Parker, Bruce, Pallister, Irwin - Kanchelskis, Ince, Keane, Giggs - Hughes, Cantona. For a start, Eric Cantona missed half the season following his kung-fu assault on the Crystal Palace fan, Matthew Simmonds, at Selhurst Park that January. But also Brucie was getting old. His aching legs just wouldn't move as quickly as they once had. And when he picked up knocks he now couldn't shake them off as easily.

And though Sir Alex initially rebuffed approaches from a rumoured "three different clubs" during 1996, convincing Bruce that he still had at least two good seasons at the top level with United still to play, the writing was on the wall as far as the then 35-year-old Brucie was concerned when he was left out of the 1996 FA Cup final which United went on to win, 1-0 against Liverpool. And in 1997, he joined promotion-chasing Birmingham City, before making the break to become a manager in his own right in 1998 with Sheffield United.

Bruce was one of many of Fergie's ex-players to make that transition into management (the list is exhausting and includes, in no particular order: Roy Keane, Bryan Robson, Gordon Strachan, Mark Hughes, Paul Ince, Steve Bruce, Darren Ferguson, Mark Robins, Henning Berg, Laurent Blanc, Chris Casper, Mike Duxbury, Frank Stapleton, Clayton Blackmore, Peter Davenport, Mike Phelan. And they're just the players played under Sir Alex at Old Trafford. It was clear clubs thought they were employing players who'd learned the United way under Fergie and they'd be ready to translate them into a new club. Bruce in particular was tipped to do well. Many observers felt his reading of the game whilst a player would make him an ideal manager. And he's done *okay* at his variety of clubs. But, a promotion at Hull City aside, he's never set the world alight like he did as a player at Old Trafford, when he practically invented the "Fergie Time" goals.

Verdict: This is a tough choice and not one I would like to make if I had to look any of this tough trio in the eyes and tell them they'd been left out. But great as Brucie's goals against Sheffield Wednesday were, and wondrous as that first title was – and it is sometimes difficult to remember just how desperate we were to lift 'the curse of twenty-six years' back in 1992-93 – the achievements of Stam, and later Vidic, leave Bruce for dust. And although Stam only played 80 games for the Reds, and although Vidic has already played over twice that, and we're still counting… And although Vida has a much better goal-scoring rate than his Dutch counterpart…

Well, there's no getting past just how good Jaap Stam actually was.

"Vidic and Bruce would both run through a brick wall for the good of the team," says Phil Martin, "but Stam was the brick wall when we won the treble!" And that, allied with his song which fans *still* sing, is the trump card here.

4 - Centre Half

To complement the zig-zagged nosed, no-nonsense, brick outhouse centre half, Ferguson's great United sides have often had a completely different type of player. A more cultured type. A centre back who is almost a Beckenbaueresque sweeper: comfortable enough on the ball to carry it out of defence, or to try a little trick. A good passer of the ball who looks to set up attacks with clever passing.

Laurent Blanc was probably Fergie's archetypal second centre half, only he arrived too late in his career to ever be considered a Fergie great, and when he did play for United, he'd lost that crucial yard of pace.

But who are the other top contenders to play this role in Fergie's finest United x11? Let's take a look…

Gary Pallister

During his nine years at United, Gary Andrew Pallister used to hitch 'em up and ride on down to the ranch (the training complex known as The Cliff) wearing cowboy boots and check shirts. On the field, he was famed for his Wild West sheriff calm, for his long, spaghetti (western) legs, and for his gallops out of defence. Off it, he was well known for his questionable fashion sense. Steve Bruce, the Tonto to Pally's Lone Ranger during their long and successful centre-back partnership, teased him mercilessly for it. And Pallister just shrugged it off. Made another perfectly timed tackle.

Gary Pallister was the man from the wild, wild north east: the plains of Middlesbrough. Though he was arguably England's most cultured defender on the pitch – and indeed, there was almost something continental, Baresi-like, about his defensive play and his reading of the game – *off* it, to say he was cultured was maybe pushing it a bit. For Pally was the type of cowboy preferred Parvo to *Pasta Arrabiata*.

He came to United in August 1989 as the most expensive British defender *ever*. His transfer was the second most costly for *any* player (behind that of Ian Rush). So no pressure there then, Pally.

In fact, Pallister's transfer was only one of many that summer, as Ferguson implemented the *spend, spend, spend* policy which has served Chelsea and Manchester City so well recently. Ferguson's intention was a wholesale revamp of the playing squad. Norman Whiteside and Paul McGrath left the club (to Everton and Villa respectively), and were replaced by Pally, Paul Ince, and Neil Webb. Ferguson turned his attentions to Pallister after missing out on the Swedish centre-back Glenn Hysen, who opted for Liverpool instead. (With hindsight, United got much, much the better player, and United have gone on to win thirteen Premier League titles since: Liverpool a grand total of none.)

The times were certainly *a-changin'* at United that summer, not only in the playing staff but also in the boardroom. Amongst much razamatazz, the property tycoon (and chancer) Michael Knighton had agreed to purchase the club from long-time owners the Edwards family. On the opening day of the season, Knighton even showed off his ball-juggling skills in front of the Stretford End, before United's new look team thrashed Arsenal 4-1.

Pallister did not play in this false dawn. He put pen to paper ten days later. By which time there were already strong rumours that Michael Knighton might not be all he seemed. And of course, we all know now that the £20 million deal for the club fell through, and the Knight-rider disappeared into the night, tail well and truly between his legs. (Knighton actually hitched up at Carlisle United: he was chairman for the club's most glorious hour – on-loan goalkeeper Jimmy Glass's last minute goal which maintained the club's league status – but also their plunge into the financial mire.)

Gary Pallister seemed bashful too in his opening performances for the Reds. Fans were left scratching their heads. It seemed inconceivable that we could have paid so much money for a player who looked so clumsy, so awkward. He resembled a new-born foal on the high plains, not quite grown into his limbs properly yet. Or else "Bambi, on ice." The nadir came at Maine Road, when a United capitulation against local rivals City (5-1) saw Pally's performance roundly booed.

And yet, there was a sense that *that* match was the making of Pally. He'd seen the bottom of the barrel. Scraped it. It couldn't get any worse. So he might as well buckle down and get on with his job. Suddenly this young foal got his nerve: began to try out his canters. And though United's league form never reached the dizzy heights it had in that opening game of the season, in the FA Cup the Reds were irresistible. The FA Cup was to become the first trophy of the Ferguson reign, but it was also the creaking open of the flood-gates. Subsequently, and over a sustained period, the Reds have won trophy after trophy.

Winning the cup gave Pally a new confidence. Playing alongside the brick wall that was Steve Bruce taught him a great deal about bravery. And, in the 1991-92 season, having Peter Schmeichel behind him helped him to refine his positioning: if he stepped out of line, Schmikes would let him know about it, in full ear-bashing detail. And though United were to ultimately miss out on the league championship in 1990-91, and in 1991-92, the defence got better and better and more trophies arrived to fill the cabinet. There was the League Cup. There was the European Cup Winners' Cup.

And then there was the apocalyptic season of 1992-93. Pallister and Bruce were like twin colossi, repelling every wave of opposition attack which threatened to crash over them. But it was in two performances *up the field* in which Pally particularly distinguished himself. First, in *that* game against Sheffield Wednesday at Old Trafford. Steve Bruce's double convinced everyone that the fates, which had conspired against the Reds for so long, had now turned. But what many fans forget is who played the ball in for Bruce's impossible winner: one Gary Andrew Pallister, who'd somehow found himself way, way behind enemy lines deep into injury time. His cross from the wide-right was perfectly timed, and placed. Lassoed itself onto Bruce's head. And the rest was history.

Second, in the match in which Reds all over the world celebrated the return of the league title to Old Trafford after twenty-six years. United faced Blackburn and, in a party atmosphere, had cruised to a 2-1 lead which could have been 6-1 were it not for some (forgivable) over-elaboration from Reds in goal-scoring positions. Then, as the clock ticked over into injury time, United won a free-kick on the edge of the Blackburn box. Usually Irwin or Cantona would have been nailed on to take it, but suddenly the United players were imploring Gary Pallister to come forward and have a crack. Pally was the only member of the team that day (apart from Schmeichel) who hadn't troubled the scorers that season, and the team saw it as the perfect opportunity for him to break his duck.

And so, up stepped our cowboy. Dead-eyed, he struck the free-kick hard and low, and unerringly into the bottom of the corner. It was the summation of an excellent and free-scoring season, and a memory which would remain with every Red for evermore.

All good things must come to an end though. Time ticked on for Pally and Bruce, the north east duo. Bruce was to leave first, in 1996, for Birmingham. And though Pallister raged against the dying of his own United light – he won his fourth Premier League title at the end of the season alongside David May or Ronny Johnsen – in 1997-98 United were dethroned by Arsenal, who took the championship by a single point, and in summer, the Prodigal Son returned to Middlesbrough for £2.5 million. Which was £200k more than United had paid for this north east cowboy all those years ago.

Rio Ferdinand

United fans might not *Love Leeds* (as the Yorkshire city's slogan goes) however we've got a lot to thank our White Rose country rivals for. Amongst all the "We all hate Leeds-scum" and "Oh Elland Road is full of sheep" chants, there are a couple of songs which are a little more *restrained*. The first is this one: "Jordan, McQueen, Cantona and Ferdinand". It's a roll-call of Red heroes who've crossed the Pennines from Leeds to United and who've become bonafide red heroes in the process. There was also, of course, Alan Smith, but his name didn't fit in...

The other chant which did the rounds in the Stretford End and K-Stand was a joyful "Leeds are our feeder club." And in a very real sense, they were. *Were.* Now they're Norwich's.

But when Rio Ferdinand signed for United from Leeds for a British record £29 million in July 2002, there was a sense United had overpaid. £29 million was a mind-boggling sum for a centre half, good as Ferdinand was. And *everyone* knew that Leeds were in financial dire straits at the time too: surely United could have shelled out another, say, £5 million, and purchased the *whole of Leeds*. We could have used Elland Road as a training ground, or as a reserve team stadium. We could have bought all of their players. And then sold them on to Bradford. Okay, we'd have kept Rio, because he was a good player, but…

Well Rio, it soon became clear, was more than just a good player. He *oozed* class. Confidence. Elegance on the ball. He was brave too. And sure, like Pallister, off the field he had his dozy moments – missing *that* drugs test in September 2003 and his *awful* car-crash TV moments in *Rio's World Cup Wind-Ups* – but Rio really was/ is the genuine article. He never seems hurried on the pitch. Always plays at his own pace. He's probably the only centre half in Britain who'll try a Cantona flick, or a pirouette – Rio was a ballet dancer at school - inside his own penalty area.

Rio came up through the same famous West Ham Academy which also produced fellow *Fergie's Greatest United x11* stars Michael Carrick and Paul Ince. At Upton Park, he made his name as a cultured central defender but one who was prone to lapses in concentration. He made the step up to Leeds though, in 2000, again for a British record transfer

77

fee (£18 million on this occasion). And it was his form in Leeds' run to the Champions League semi-finals in 2001 that convinced Fergie he'd left those concentration-lapses behind and could perform at the highest level.

And the cockney centre-back's first season seemed to bear out Fergie's faith in him: United carried off the Premier League championship that year. But in 2003, disaster struck. Rio had neglected to attend a scheduled drugs test at Carrington, deciding instead to go into Manchester, shopping. His 'lapse in concentration' was to land him with an *eight month* ban from football by the FA. It was to be the start of a tempestuous relationship between Rio and English football's governing body which took in the John Terry affair, Rio's being dropped by England, and Rio's subsequent refusal of a call-up by the England manager Roy Hodgson. Many United fans maintain that Rio was harshly treated by England, and the FA, and were genuinely pleased at Rio's decision not to represent the national side in 2013. United fans have always felt the club are "bigger than England", and that the Reds have been treated with undue severity by the FA in matters of suspensions and discipline.

On his return to the side after an eight month ban, Ferdinand shrugged off initial ring-rustiness and began to show his best form again. He helped the team to claim the League Cup in 2005-06, and then, in the following season, he won his second Premier League winner's medal. The 2007–08 season however, was possibly his best in a Red shirt (although 2012-13 runs it close). That season, he started like a train. The whole defence did: they kept six consecutive clean sheets in the league in September-October and were cruising in the Champions League. Come January and they began their FA Cup campaign, and this was also progressing well. Hopes began to be raised of a repeat of the 1999 treble. But then, in the FA Cup quarter-final against Portsmouth at Old Trafford, the train went off the rails. Van Der Sar suffered an injury and had to be replaced by the Polish substitute Tomasz Kuszczak. And then things got even worse when Kuszczak was sent off in conceding a penalty. It was Rio opted to go in goal for the Reds. And though he got close to Sulley Muntari's penalty, he didn't get close enough. United were out of the FA Cup and the treble was off the menu.

A grand double was still on, however, and Rio, as United's captain, was to ensure there were no more slip-ups. The Reds wrapped up the league title in some style, and then it was off to Moscow for the Champions League final against Premier League rivals Chelsea. And after an open first hour in which both teams attacked at will, the defences – and particularly Rio – began to take control. The score at the end of normal time was 1-1, and so fans had the agonising additional half-hour of Extra Time. But *still* neither defence could be breached. And so it was penalties… And then, when even the first five penalties each couldn't separate the teams, *sudden death* penalties. But then Giggs scored, and Van Der Sar saved Anelka's penalty, and Rio had his proudest moment. He, along with Ryan Giggs, lifted the big Champions League trophy aloft in the Moscow air and United fans were in raptures.

All that heavy lifting didn't do Rio any favours. From 2009-10 through to 2011-12, his United career was injury plagued. Fergie began to use him more sparingly; managing Ferdinand's back and knee problems by sitting him out for the less important matches. An indication of the esteem in which Fergie still held Rio though, was in the fact he was still an automatic pick for the A-games. And Rio still picked up a Premier League winner's medal in 2010-11 (as of 2012-13,   he has six.)

In 2012-13, almost miraculously, Rio's niggling injuries abated somewhat, and he played far more matches than he'd done in nearly five seasons. The regular games meant his consistency returned, and his form was exceptional as United set about trying to wrestle back the Premier League crown from the "noisy neighbours", Manchester City. The image of him, celebrating in grand style after Robin Van Persie's last minute winner at the Etihad Stadium, was typical of the man. He always loved his celebrations. Always seemed to risk life and limb (and back and knee) by launching himself on top of the other players. But in that Manchester City celebration, Rio was hit by a coin, thrown by a City fan. Rio was left with a cut above his eyebrow. He bled Red.

And this injury seemed to drive him on to ever greater feats during the rest of the season as United steamrollered opposition from Newcastle to Southampton. Reclaiming the league from Manchester City after the agony of Sergio Aguero's last gasp winner in May 2012 was the number one priority for United fans, staff, and players. And you got the impression that Rio was so determined to achieve this he *ignored* his injuries.

And on Monday 22nd April 2013, when a 3-0 victory against Aston Villa guaranteed United the crown, it was Rio partying harder than anyone else on the pitch, even those younger colleagues for whom this was their first league title win. There was Rio, performing that odd, high-stepping run all the way across the old Trafford pitch, draped in a United Champions: 20 flag. There was Rio, leading the team choir. There was Rio dancing, really dancing.

Thanks, Leeds.

Phil Jones

In 2012-13, United are lucky enough to boast a crop of young defenders who could go on to be the best collective unit in the club's history. There's Rafael, of course, and Jonny Evans. There's Chris Smalling, and then there's Phil Jones. Jones blends the skill and comfort on the ball of a Rio Ferdinand, with the muscle of a Vidic and the bulk of a Stam. Jones *just might* have everything.

In the wake of the 2012-13 Premier League title triumph, Fergie was often asked to compare and contrast his best United sides, just as we're doing here. Obviously he spoke glowingly of Robin Van Persie, whose signature proved to be *one* of the deciding factors in the title ending up in M16 rather than M11. And he spoke in awed tones of Ryan Giggs and the records he'd set. But he also spoke of his hopes for the future. And those hopes seemed to be embodied in one man. Phil Jones.

Sir Alex truly believes that Jonesy has it in him to become the "greatest" ever United player. He said: "I think Jones may be one of the best players we have ever signed. He has such a massive influence, instinct, reading of the game. He has a drive about him."

Drive is, of course, one of the main qualities Fergie sought out in a player. He looked in their eyes and strove to discover that hunger which would drive them on to look for equalisers and winners when everyone else has given up. And he recognised this in Jones. Phil Jones who, at the age of nineteen, was already being picked out as a future England captain. Phil Jones who, in hushed, reverential tones, is sometimes spoken of in the same sentence – but not the same breath – as the great Duncan Edwards.

Phil Jones arrived at United from Blackburn in the summer of 2011 and made an instant impact with his rampaging runs and his lion-heartedness. His sheer versatility was also seen as a massive plus. Jones has played in numerous positions for the Reds, and for the moment, he seems most at home at right-back, or else at centre half. He's also impressed as a specialist defensive midfielder though - as witnessed in his man-marking jobs on opponents as tricky as Cristiano Ronaldo. If the player can steer clear of injuries, his future could be outstanding.

Certainly nobody can top him in the 'gurning' stakes. Gurning contests are something of a tradition, particularly in Lancashire towns, and the Preston-born Jones has already proved himself a dyed-in-the-wool gurner: his 'determined', 'pained' and 'angry' facial contortions trend on Twitter on a weekly basis.

Verdict: It's too early for Jones, good though he is. And Pallister is trumped by Ferdinand on account of Rio's Champions League winner's medal, and the fact that Rio is a higher class of player: the Merc to Pally's Ford Focus. Mind you, it's probably not wise to use the word "Merk" in Rio's hearing unless you actually liked his *World Cup Wind-Ups* show.

Neil Custis, who covers Manchester United and Manchester City for *The Sun* newspaper, says: "The centre-half position will have created much debate. For me you have to take it as a partnership. So is it Bruce and Pallister or Vidic and Ferdinand. For me it is the latter because I believe they are not just quality defenders but use the ball so well. Ferdinand is also the best reader of a game of all four."

And though Stam has *just* edged ahead of Vidic in 'Team Fergie', Ferdinand's place is nailed-on. Rio scored his first goal in five years for the Reds, three minutes from the end of the match against Swansea, on May 12th 2013. It was Sir Alex Ferguson's last home match as United manager, and Rio had just given him the most fitting of send-offs.

5 - Left Full-Back

Gone are the days when 'left-back' used to be the punchline of a joke (i.e. 'What position do you play?' 'Left-back.' 'What, like left back in the changing room?') The left full-back role at United is a crucial cog in the engineering of the team.

Arguably, the United left full-back has the most space to exploit of any other player on the team. They're well away from the congested midfield area and have much of the left flank to call their own, particularly when their winger cuts inside. At United, the left-back role is thus one characterised by hard running. Our left-backs require an Energiser-bunny quality with which to keep bounding up and down the pitch: one moment they are supplementing an attack, the next careering back to help out the defence.

There are two stand-out nominations for the role of left full-back in 'Team Fergie', and we'll consider their merits now:

Patrice Evra

Sir Alex Ferguson's distrust of players available in the January transfer window was a characteristic of the later years of his managerial career. Sure there have been a few occasions when United have snapped up a young player: 'one for the future'. But big money splashes *a la* Torres to Chelsea and Andy Carroll to Liverpool have been conspicuous by their absence.

However, in January 2006, United brought in not one, but two players to increase cover in defensive positions. Nemanja Vidic arrived from Spartak Moscow for £7 million, and a certain Patrice Evra, for £5.5 million from Monaco. It soon became clear that Vidic, the big Serb centre back, wasn't just going to be defensive cover, but a mainstay of the team. Evra, however, made a less impressive start.

Evra's debut came in the Manchester derby, away at the new City of Manchester Stadium. Although a daunting start, it was an ideal opportunity for the left-back to set out his stall for a proper place in the team. Things couldn't have gone more wrong. Evra looked out-of-his-depth: positionally unaware, shaky on the ball, and encountering numerous 'communication problems' with his teammates, he was hooked at half-time by Sir Alex. Judging from his performance, fans could have been forgiven for reminding the manager that there was a good reason he usually shunned the cut-throat January transfer window.

But Evra soon proved he was made of sterner stuff. Patrice had always had to fight to stand out from the crowd. Growing up, he was one of 25 (and like the vidiprinter when an especially high score rolls in, I'll also confirm that in words - *twenty-five*) siblings. Born in Senegal, his family moved to a Paris suburb when Patrice was a toddler. (He's gone on to win - at the time of publication - 48 caps for France.) He joined United to fight for the full-back berth with firm fans' favourite, the Argentinian hardman Gabriel Heinze, and French compatriot Mikael Silvestre. And at first it seemed as though Patrice would be the certain loser. However, he made slow, steady progress, and in his second season, his excellent displays and positive running gradually convinced Ferguson to make him his first-choice left-back.

Since then, Evra's not looked back. In the now frequent absences of Nemanja Vidic through injury and 'body-management', Patrice Evra's been made captain of the team, and he's proved himself as staunchly United as Manchester boys like the Nevilles, Butt, Scholes and Danny Welbeck. He's a veritable rentaquote when it comes to talking-up the Reds, and, as far as fans are concerned, he says all the right things.

Here's Evra on what set his pulse racing on joining United: "When I arrived here people asked me what excited me most. I said it was not training with Ronaldo and Wayne Rooney but players like Giggs and Scholes."

And here he is on the way things are run at the club: "United is a completely different world; they take care of the tiniest detail for you. To be honest, I'll be the king of all c**ts if I can't be a success under such conditions."

And finally, my all-time favourite Evra-ism: "Any agent asking for a transfer request for Cristiano Ronaldo would have to come with a bazooka."

Patrice is a prickly character all right. He's been involved in numerous controversies, not least his role in the 'walk-out' of the French squad in the 2010 World Cup. Then there have been his run-ins with ground-staff at Chelsea ('lawnmowergate'), and his many snipes at Arsenal. Often these incidents have been in, or after, matches with United's big rivals and this has endeared him to United fans.

Of course the biggest controversy of the lot was the Luis Suarez affair. And it was here that the France full-back really showed his class. So much has been written about the original incident – Suarez's racial abuse of Evra – that I won't scrape the barrel to go into it here. Suffice to say it was disgusting. Something which should never, ever happen on a football pitch or anywhere else in the world. However what I would like to focus on is the dignity with which Evra handled the aftermath when a whole lot of muck was being slung his way.

Liverpool FC representatives, ex-players, and many commentators cast aspersions on Patrice's character. They called him a liar. They said he "had form". But throughout it all, Evra kept quiet. He reacted in the right way: on the pitch. And then, when Suarez added insult to injury with his refusal to shake hands in the corresponding United-Liverpool fixture at Old Trafford, Evra still held his tongue.

He only showed the full weight of his feelings on the matter twice. Once *after* that United-Liverpool clash in which United had won, and his celebrations were criticised for being somewhat over-exuberant (well hell, didn't they *deserve* to be) and then, at the end of the 2012-13 season when United had walked the title and the players were completing a lap of honour on the Old Trafford turf. Some wag in the crowd had somehow smuggled a prosthetic arm into the stadium – and that's some smuggle! – and, as Evra passed, tossed it onto the field of play. Evra picked up the arm and pretended to gnaw on the thing, referring to another Suarez incident in which he'd bitten the Chelsea player Branislav Ivanovic. It was a witty, classy comeback from Evra, and one which was greeted with widespread delight from the Red faithful.

Evra's indefegatability is a key aspect of his character *on the field* too. He is hardly ever injured, despite encountering full-blooded challenges on a weekly basis. Indeed, there are times when Patrice seems to be rubber-limbed. A defender will smash into him and he'll simply bounce back up and continue with his run. It was the former Crystal Palace manager Iain Dowie first coined the term "bouncebackability". It was supposed to describe Palace's ability to 'bounce back' after defeats. Patrice Evra *embodies* "bouncebackability". He has it in spades. This is one man whose Tubthumping displays mean he gets "knocked down, but he gets up again" time and time again.

Evra began his career as an attacking midfielder, before being shunted to left-back by Monaco, a club he represented in the 2004 Champions League Final (where they lost to Mourinho's Porto). However, he's lost none of his attacking flair when pressed into his now more defensive role. Indeed his swashbuckling runs out of defence, as well as his "bouncebackability" have been a key aspect of his play at United. He excels with over-lapping runs, working in tandem with whatever winger is playing in front of him; be it Giggs, Nani, or Young.

Recently, he has also added goal-scoring to his menu. His clever runs at corner kicks have offered United a new attacking dimension from corner kicks in the 2012-13 season - a season United trumped every other Premier League club in terms of goals scored from corners. This is some promotion for the left-back: in previous seasons Evra was hardly ever called upon to come forward for set-plays – probably on account of his size – and was generally the man to hang back on the half-way line at corners, marking the opposition's speed-merchant in case of a break.

2012-13 has been Evra's best season for three or four years. In it, he's shown the ability to "bounce back" from all kinds of adversity both on and off the field. Geed up by the arrival of the Dutch left-back, Alexander Buttner, he has played his way back into form and he has reminded United fans of just how good he was in his pomp.

Neutral commentators often point to Ashley Cole of Chelsea when asked to name the best left full-back in the Premier League over the past few seasons. Perhaps the reason for this is because a great many of these 'neutrals' are English. And though Cole has been excellent, let it be said that the vast majority of United fans would not swap Patrice Evra for anyone else, this or any season.

Evra has had a glittering career at United. His personal trophy cabinet includes five Premier League winner's medals, three League Cup winner's medals, one Champions League winner's medal, and one FIFA World Club Cup winner's medal. He's played well over 300 competitive matches for the Reds and shows no signs of slowing up. In fact, any agent who endeavoured to try and get Evra to move on from the club he loves might have to come armed with a bazooka. And perhaps even then, even after the bazooka was fired, Patrice might well just bounce straight back up again.

Denis Irwin

It's the big money buys that make the headlines. United smashing the transfer record on a top striker, for example, or breaking the bank to land a goal-scoring midfielder. But often it's the transfer dealings at the bottom end of the market - the bargain basement buys as we've already seen with Schmeichel and Van der Sar - which are the mark of a top manager with an eye for a player.

Denis Irwin arrived at United for a paltry £625,000 from Oldham Athletic in 1990. His

sterling performances for the Latics in the 1990 FA
Cup Semi Final - in which they took United to a
replay at Maine Road before Mark Robins, inevitably
that season, scored a scruffy winner for the reds -
convinced Fergie to 'sign him up.'

Sir Alex can hardly have made a more cost-
effective signing in his entire United career. For
Irwin was a loyal servant: he stayed at United for 12
years, winning 7 Premier League titles, 3 FA Cups, 1
League Cup, and, of course, the big one, the
Champions League. Over the period, he scored 22
league goals, and 4 Champions League goals, and,
most impressively, 7 in the FA Cup (in only 43
games). Some total for a full-back. To put this in
some perspective, on the right hand side of the
defence, Gary Neville scored only 7 goals in his
entire United career (which stood at over 600
games).

Denis Irwin was nerveless from the penalty
spot and, when he held penalty-taking duties, his
record was 8 out of 10, or 80%. (Wayne Rooney's
success rate is 65%). He was dubbed 'Mr.
Consistency' by fans due to this record, and the fact
he was so often rewarded with 7s or 8s out of 10 in
the *Manchester Evening News*' player ratings. In fact,

the Irishman could have started his own *Mr. Man* range: he was also dubbed "Mr. Dependable" by no less than Sir Alex Ferguson.

But if all this number-crunching, all this talk of consistency and dependability, hasn't convinced, what about Irwin's lasting impact upon the *souls* of United fans? What role did he play in those memories which will last a lifetime?

Well, in the wonderful 2009 Ken Loach film *Looking for Eric,* Eric the footballer is asked by Eric the postman to name his "sweetest moment" ever as a United player. Fittingly, Cantona does not pick one of his own goals, but instead one by Denis Irwin against Tottenham in a home league game in January 1993. The goal, which is set up by an outrageous Cantona-flick which loops over the entire Spurs defence, remains one of the most beautiful scored in Ferguson's reign, summing up everything about the philosophy this United team had - the majesty of it. They were desperate to win the league after so long, and yet they weren't going to simply grind their way to the title. They were going to win it in glorious attacking style. Even their full-backs were stylish.

And how. Irwin was a cultured player. His free-kicks were of a sustained quality only Beckham and Ronaldo have matched in United colours. He could give life to a dead ball with the subtlety and effectiveness of noted specialists such as Juninho Pernambuca and Sinisa Mihajlovic. His runs down the left flank were penetrating, and his passing was of a higher level to that generally expected from a full-back. Indeed, there is an argument to say that Irwin, in his own quiet way, reinvented the full-back role for the modern era. With his rich blend of both attacking and defensive work, he set out the new parameters in order that players like Evra, and Ashley Cole, could flourish.

Irwin was awarded a testimonial for United, recognising a decade's service for the Reds. It was held at Old Trafford in summer 2000, against Manchester City. Unfortunately, the match wasn't as friendly as it should have been, and Irwin himself had to be substituted in the first half after a terrible attempted tackle by City's Weah. His absence from most of his own testimonial seemed typical of this 'Mister Quiet', and yet the real testimonial for his United career came in competitive matches. In 2001, he went on to win his seventh Premier League winner's medal with the Reds, proving that after all, the *Mister Man* he really should have been was 'Mister Winner'. Denis was a born winner. Hell, even his name ends with the word 'win'. And that's the final word on the matter.

Verdict: Evra. By a nose. The Irishman runs him close though, especially because Irwin's goal-scoring rate was so much more impressive. But Patrice's noise wins it for him. His sheer, boisterous United-ness sets him apart. Evra had to learn English when he first came to these shores, but he also swotted-up on Manchester United Football Club. And he's proved a brilliant student. He knows exactly what the club *means*. And he knows exactly how to conduct himself as a United hero. Not only has he consistently outshone Luis Suarez in terms of medals, he has also proved better than him at behaving like a human being.

Neil Custis agrees: "Left-back is between Evra and Irwin. Many would go for Irwin for consistency and longevity. But Evra at his very best, was the world's best in that position. Not only an incredible defender but a force going forward and also a very influential figure in the camp.

And it was Evra who again showed his class on Sunday 12th May when United collected their final trophy of Sir Alex's reign. The Frenchman, along with club captain Vidic, passed up the opportunity to lift the trophy himself and instead handed it over to Fergie to do the honours. And the image of Sir Alex lifting the Premier League trophy will remain with those who saw it forever.

6 - Right-Wing

Fergie's penchant for racehorses is well documented. And on United's right-wing, we've borne witness to a number of thoroughbred performers over the years. There've been the canterers, like Andrei Kanchelskis and Antonio Valencia, show-ponies like Luis Nani, and destriers – a word derived from the Latin for right-sided - like David Beckham.

Then there's Cristiano Ronaldo, who comes in a category all of his own. Ronaldo, so often accused of being a flat-track bully (or again, a show-pony) early in his career, has now proved himself to be the real deal.

Here we'll put some of the leading candidates for the honour of being Ferguson's best United right-winger through their paces.

Andrei Kanchelskis

There were no transfer windows back in 1991, so when a certain Ukranian-born Russian winger signed for £650,000 towards the end of March, he rather slipped under the radar. There was none of the manufactured razzmatazz we get from Sky TV today on deadline day, when they send a phalanx of reporters to shiver outside semi-deserted training grounds for hours on end, looking increasingly nervous as they're surrounded by mob of local kids desperate to shout a TV hello to their mums. There was no Jim White yelling some hastily prepared, but enthusiastically delivered, stats about United's new boy - he comes from Shaktar Donetsk, he plays on the right - into a boom-mic whilst at the same time desperately seeking out the tail-lights of any car driving past in case the new signing was being secreted into the Cliff under cover of darkness.

There was no Youtube. Fans couldn't look up this 'Andrei whatwasit?' on the web, and discover countless examples of blurry footage from some Eastern European outposts in which he showcased his crack skills. Nobody but nobody seemed to know anything about the supposed 'Russian star'.

101

And besides, the thoughts of those same supporters were, at the time, consumed with on-pitch matters. The business-end of the season was fast approaching and the Reds were progressing very well in the European Cup Winners' Cup (they'd eventually reach the final, in Rotterdam, where they saw off Barcelona) and United were still fighting for a decent finish in the league (they'd eventually finish sixth).

So Andrei Kanchelskis was hardly a signing who set the pulse racing. And indeed, after he signed, he seemed to disappear completely, as though he was an agent gone deep undercover. Kanchelskis didn't even make the squad for that heady night in Holland, when Hughes' goals won the club their second European trophy, and when his debut did arrive, it was in a meaningless end of season game against Crystal Palace at Selhurst Park in which the Reds, shockingly, lost 3-0.

But United's new right-winger, the man who'd slipped under the Iron Curtain, was to explode onto the scene the following season. It was as though he'd spent the previous months carefully compiling a dossier of intel: about United, his fellow players, the opposition. In the 1991-92 season, Agent Andrei played in 34 out of the 42 league games, scoring five goals, as United fought tooth and nail to rid themselves of the albatross which had clung to our collective necks for twenty-six years. Fans were hungry for success. We'd tasted glory with the FA Cup win in 1990, and, the following year, the Cup Winners' Cup. Now we wanted the big one. The league championship.

The 1991-92 season was a story of glorious failure, with the reds starting to play in an all-out attacking style which brought to mind the teams of the sixties. The Reds attacked relentlessly down the wings, and Andrei was a key member of the side. He was as fast and as direct as a horse on the flat. Powerful too. He ran like a train, like the Trans-Siberian Express, leading rapier-like counters. If there was one criticism, it was that he was *too* direct. He had a tendency to run up blind alleys, or in some cases, off the pitch. But we loved him. Sung his name over and over to the tune of *Hava Nagila*. Performed impromptu Cossack dances in the Stretford End.

And yet, glorious failure was still failure. The agony of missing out to our bitter rivals from over the Pennines, Leeds United, in the fight to become the last ever winners of the English First Division was almost unbearable. Though United eventually won their first ever League Cup, by beating Nottingham Forest at Wembley with a goal from Brian McClair, it seemed as though we'd *never* win the league again. But Ferguson, as is his wont, took that heartbreak, that despair, and he turned it into something else. He used it to forge a new, unbreakable spirit within the team which meant that next season there was *absolutely no way* the players would let the league trophy slip through their fingers again.

The United team that graced the first ever Premier League season - a false-start in their opening match against Sheffield United and an early inability to kill teams off notwithstanding - burned with a desire to win, and win well. They had no mercy. However, Agent Andrei's career hit something of a standstill. Lee Sharpe returned from a long-term injury and took the Russian's place for much of the second half of the season. But in 1993-94, Kanchelskis stepped up to the plate as the team began to play with a new swagger as befitting their status as champions. United won the double that year and Andrei was a crucial member of the dream-team (Schmeichel - Parker, Bruce, Pallister, Irwin - Kanchelskis, Ince, Keane, Giggs - Hughes, Cantona) which barely lost a game when they played together.

Unfortunately, that x11 didn't all play as often as they should have. There were a lot of hard men in that side. A lot who could succumb to the red-mist. Frequent suspensions meant Fergie was forced to tinker. Kanchelskis himself was sent off in the League Cup final against Aston Villa for a handball on the goal-line. Against ten men, Villa went on to secure a 3–1 victory, and United lost their chance to become the only English club to win a domestic treble.

The next season, Agent Andrei set about single-handedly trying to make up for the disappointment on missing out on the domestic treble. He finished as leading goalscorer, with 14 in the league alone. Amongst those goals was a famous hat-trick against Manchester City at Old Trafford, in a resounding 5-0 win. Kanchelskis remains the last United player to score a hat-trick in this fixture, and for this he will be forever a Red Hero. (He'd also go on to become the answer to that tough quiz question - which player has scored in a Manchester, Merseyside, and Glasgow derby?)

However, the 1994-95 season was doomed to ultimate failure as injuries and suspensions - that perennial worry of this brilliant United side - caught up with them. Andrei himself suffered a hernia at the business-end of the season - at a time when Eric Cantona had been suspended for eight months after his kung-fu attack on the Crystal Palace fan, Matthew Simmonds - and United stuttered, allowing Blackburn Rovers to pip the Reds at the post and carry off the Premier League title.

We didn't know it then, but Andrei's hat-trick against our local rivals was the beginning of the end for him at the club. As it was for a number of other key players, as Ferguson ruthlessly set about rebuilding the side, ready for a new assault on the title. Club stalwarts Ince and Hughes were sold, and then, at the last, Agent Andrei also left, for Everton. In his autobiography, Ferguson wrote about the unconventional, and rather distasteful, nature of the transfer. Agent Andrei's agent was apparently very threatening. Apparently, there were guns brought in to contract negotiations. And so Andrei left.

The summer of 1995 seemed a rather dark time to be a United fan. Of course, in hindsight, we can see the wisdom of Fergie's cull of such important senior players. Sir Alex kept coming out in the press, claiming everything would work out fine.

Apparently there were a set of youngsters better than his Fledglings of the late eighties, early nineties, waiting in the wings for their chance.

Little did we know just how right Fergie would be proved.

David Beckham

David Robert Joseph Beckham was one of the young tyros tasked with keeping United feasting from the top table fans had become accustomed to dining from. A cockney with a penchant for curtained hair and fast cars – one of his first acts on being offered a new contract during his early years at United was to buy Ryan Giggs' old car, a souped-up Escort – he was seen by some as a little on the flash side, however those 'in the know' at the club knew all about his dedication and superlative work ethic. They also knew about his supreme skills with a dead ball, and about the excellence of his crossing. Though he lacked the devastating pace of a typical United winger, he more than made up for this with his innate ability to place a ball on a sixpence, or, in this case, on the head of a United striker.

Most importantly, those 'in the know' knew all about Beckham's Red credentials. His father, Ted, was a die-hard United fan. Beckham himself had attended the Bobby Charlton Soccer School and had wowed coaches with his ball-juggling skills. He loved everything about United, and wore the shirt as though it was the biggest honour in the world.

With the benefit of hindsight, we all know the narrative of Beckham's seemingly inexorable rise to international superstardom. We know all about his celebrity marriage. The endorsements. The films named in his honour. We know how he's become like the Beatles and conquered America, and now how he hobnobs with A-list stars: he counts Tom Cruise amongst his closest pals, dontchaknow. We can read about all of this stuff in the pages of *Hello* magazine. But what's so touching about Becks – and yeah, it was United fans first called him Becks, *not Hello,* thank you very much – is that, despite all the distractions (more on that later), despite the wealth, despite the international jetsetting lifestyle, is the fact that he retains such obvious affection for Manchester United Football Club. I mean, the guy can barely go an interview – even *with Hello* – in which he doesn't talk about United.

David Beckham wears his Red heart on his sleeve. Maybe you can't quite spot it under all the tattoos, but it is there, and it will be forever more.

From the very beginning, we've seen the pure, boyish enthusiasm Becks exhibits when playing for, talking about, or watching United. We've tracked his career from the very early days, when he lived in digs in Manchester and felt homesick for his Essex home. We feel almost paternal towards him. We stood up for him, allowed him to keep his head when all of England was losing theirs after he departed the 1998 World Cup in disgrace, having been sent-off against Argentina for a silly flick of his leg against Diego Simeone. We chanted his name when effigies of the young starlet were being hung from lamp-posts outside pubs in his native East End of London. We gave him rapturous applause – more acclaim than we afforded even those in red shirts – when he returned to Old Trafford with one of his new clubs, AC Milan.

We loved him because throughout his long and lavishly successful career, a career in which he eventually collected as many clubs as Colin

Montgomerie, he maintained he'd never play for another English club after Manchester United. Because he admitted Manchester United was the pinnacle, the top of the mountain, and *after* United, there was only one way: down. Because he knew he'd feel dirty, like a cheating husband, if he were ever expected to wear the shirt of another English team.

Of course, Becks *did* wear the shirt of another English team. Though he'd made a couple of first-team appearances, including a Champions League debut against Galatasaray in a 4-0 win in 1994 in which he scored, appearances were at a premium for the young cockney. And, as has become customary, Ferguson sent Becks out on loan in order to gain some much-needed experience. In 1995, Beckham shipped-up at Preston North End, where he was to enjoy a decent run in the team, playing alongside Fergie's replacement as United manager, David Moyes. At Preston, Beckham showed the finesse, allied with fire, which we all came to know and love at United. He also exhibited his eye for the spectacular, prefacing his later goal from his own half against Wimbledon for the Reds, by scoring directly from a corner for the Lilywhites.

Beckham returned to United in April 1995, and was rewarded with four first team appearances. Unfortunately, his return coincided with United's disastrous end to the season in which the Reds lost out to Blackburn Rovers in the race for the title, and then to Everton in the FA Cup Final. It was the first year since 1989 in which United had finished a season trophyless. And the fans' despair at this state of affairs was hardly lessened by a turbulent summer in which three senior players – Hughes, Ince, and Kanchelskis – were all sold, and yet no new signings were made. Ferguson, it seemed, was putting his faith in 'the kids'.

Such faith seemed misguided on the opening day of the 1995-96 season, when United went down 3-1 to Aston Villa at Villa Park (Beckham scored). It was a performance which gave rise to Alan Hansen's notorious comment on *Match of the Day:* "You'll never win anything with kids." Beckham, along with those other now world-renowned promotees from United's youth team – Gary and Phil Neville, Ryan Giggs, Nicky Butt, Paul Scholes – was to spend much of the rest of the season, indeed, much of the rest of his career, ramming those words firmly down Hansen's throat.

That year, United won the League and FA Cup double. The league title was delivered against all the odds: United recovered an astounding ten point deficit on Kevin Keegan's Newcastle United to carry home the trophy. As to the FA Cup, Becks scored the winner in the semi-final, against Chelsea at Villa Park, and was interviewed post-match. And this, remember, was before his PR polish. He came out blushing; self-conscious, could barely string a sentence together. Eventually, in squeaky cockney, he managed to describe his goal. Self-effacingly, he admitted: "It 'it a bobble." The final was even sweeter, as United's kids – spearheaded by the old master Cantona – defeated their white-suit-wearing Liverpool counterparts, the so-called "Spice Boys" thanks to a very late goal from Eric.

However, 1996-97 was the season David Beckham truly announced himself to the footballing world. On the opening day of the season, against Wimbledon, our number 10 collected the ball in his own half at Selhurst Park. He took a couple of touches to steady himself. Looked up. Everyone present – fans, players, staff – must have thought he was readying himself to pick out a trademark long pass. He wasn't. Becks was checking the positioning of Wimbledon's goalkeeper, Neil Sullivan. Sullivan, he noticed, was quite a long way off his line. And yet, Becks was standing on the halfway line. It would take some audacity to take a shot…

And yet, that's exactly what Becks did. He sent a teasing, floating, guided-missile of a shot spearing over Sullivan's head and into the back of the net. And in one strike of the ball, became an icon. The great Pele had tried a similar shot in the 1972 World Cup, only he'd missed. Our own David Beckham had scored.

From that moment on, there was no looking back for Becks. He took on United's fabled number 7 shirt after Eric Cantona's departure, following such Red luminaries as George Best and Steve Coppell. He became an increasingly important player to the team. Beckham wasn't particularly blessed with pace, but he could caress a ball better than anybody in England at the time, and his crossing produced a huge number of goals for the Reds. This skill was, of course, down to Becks' innate ability, but it was an ability he honed and improved. For years, he'd been putting in extra practice on the training ground alongside Eric Cantona. Now it was beginning to pay off.

Though 1997-98 was a disappointing season for the Reds. Looking back through the lens of history, it was like one huge summoning of the collective Red breath before the superhuman exertions of the following year. United finished second, to a rejuvenated Arsenal, led by the hitherto unknown French manager Arsene Wenger. And this year it was United's turn to be hauled back after amassing a huge points league over their North London rivals. Arsenal went on to win the double that year, and, under Wenger's canny stewardship, would go on to provide serious competition for the Reds for much of the next decade.

The increased level of competition also served to ensure United upped their game. And in 1998-99, they battled it out on both European and domestic fronts with a renewed focus and energy. Beckham too had a point to prove. When the season started, opposing fans wouldn't let him forget his indiscretions in an England shirt in the 1998 World Cup. He'd become a hate figure. Who could forget those headlines after England's exit to Argentina? This from *The Mirror*: "Ten Heroic Lions and One Stupid Boy".

Well, in 1998-99, David Beckham became a man. Like the team he strained heart and nerve and sinew for the cause, never relenting, as United powered towards a unique treble coronation. Becks played a crucial role in the delivery of the Premier League title. He played in 34 of the 38 games, scoring six goals, including the all-important equalizer against Tottenham Hotspur in the final game of the season, a match United went on to win 2-1, thus ensuring they pipped Arsenal at the post.

The run to the FA Cup final was no less fraught with tension. In the Fourth Round, United were drawn at home to Liverpool, and were one down with the match approaching injury time. But, in an amazing precursor to the Champions League final heroics, United came back from the brink, with Yorke, and then Solksjaer (who else?) bringing United back from the brink. The quarter-finals were no easier for the Reds. Having drawn at home to Chelsea (Paul Scholes was sent off), United were taken to a tricky replay at Stamford Bridge. Two goals from Yorke secured their place in the semi-finals.

The FA Cup semi-finals of 1998-99 proved two of the most archetypal games of the Ferguson era. We had the great opposition – and make no mistake, that Arsenal side were very, very good. We had the great venue – Villa Park. Semi-finals are so much *better* played at proper semi-final venues, rather than at Wembley, as they are today. We had the thrills, we had the spills. We met those "two imposters", "Triumph and Disaster", in the same game. This was football at its gut-clenching, fist-pumping, heart-stopping best.

The first game finished as a tight 0-0 draw and this match became the last ever FA Cup semi-final to go to a replay. *And what a way to finish…* The replay was a pulsating game. End-to-end stuff. The match is famous now for THE Giggs goal and THAT hairy-chested celebration. But the match was about so much more. It was about belief. It was about Schmeichel's amazing penalty save. It was about United overcoming, even after Roy Keane's sending-off. There was a sense that destiny called that April evening: had Arsenal gone on to win, they'd likely have walked off with the Premier League trophy as well, and United might well have stumbled in the Champions League. But the 1999 United weren't for stumbling. This was the team dreams were made of, and that year, they were to walk with kings. It's often forgotten, buried under the tumult of admiration for the Giggs goal, that Beckham scored the opening goal of the game, in the seventeenth minute. Yet another critical contribution to United's best ever year from our number 7.

United went on to win the FA Cup in 1999, in a forgettable game against Newcastle at Wembley, with goals from Sheringham and Scholes, but, given what was to come a few days later, in Barcelona, United fans were simply glad of a game which didn't see the nails shredded and the nerves jangled for ninety minutes.

Due to the suspensions of United's central midfield lynchpins, Scholes and Keane, Beckham was asked to play an unaccustomed role in the Champions League final. United would miss his pinpoint crossing throughout a ninety minutes in which they struggled to create a single chance, as German giants Bayern Munich looked certain to win the trophy after taking a very early lead through Mario Basler. Indeed, Bayern missed countless opportunities of their own to put the game out of sight, with the big striker Carsten Jancker smashing a shot against the bar and Scholl and Effenberg missing presentable chances.

Some Munich players were already imagining lifting the famous big trophy. When Lothar Matthaus was substituted in the eightieth minute, he mimed lifting the trophy to the delight of the German fans. For them, it was simply a matter of waiting out time.

They'd clearly not read the script. They'd clearly not reckoned on the sheer number of late goals United had scored that season. They'd not realised just how single-minded United were to bring the trophy back to Old Trafford on the very day we celebrated the late Sir Matt Busby's birthday.

"Can Manchester United score?" asked Clive Tyldesley, "Manchester United always score."

The match was just ticking over into injury time when United won a corner. As Beckham prepared to take it, TV cameras homed in on the mad dash of goalkeeper Peter Schmeichel as he thundered forward, hoping to create havoc in the opposition's box.

For once, Beckham's corner wasn't brilliant. It missed the Great Dane, but fell kindly for Dwight Yorke, lurking with intent over the other side of the penalty area. Yorke knocked it back in and a game of pinball commenced: Bayern unable to clear properly, United's forwards unable to apply a proper touch on the ball. A sliced clearance reached Ryan Giggs on the edge of the box. *He* miscued. Somehow, the ball wormed its way to Teddy Sheringham, on as a late substitute. Sheringham stabbed a foot at the ball… And saw it nestling in the corner of the net.

The match looked destined to go into extra time, but, with the Bayern players reeling in the wake of the equalizer, United forged forward again. Won another corner. This time the clock had ticked round to the ninety-second minute. Beckham *again* took the set-play, and this time his corner was more accurate. Sheringham headed it on, Solksjaer stuck out a toe and Manchester United "reached the promised land."

That both goals stemmed from Beckham corners was telling, a fitting testimony to his performances throughout the season. He was also recognised when it came to the glitzy end of season awards ceremonies, finishing runner-up to Barcelona's Rivaldo in the European Footballer of the Year award.

The following season, United, and Becks, played like true champions. The Red Devils *walked* the Premier League, eventually winning it by eighteen points. They won all eleven of their final matches, with Beckham in scintillating form, scoring five times in this period.

But, despite the fact everything appeared rosy at Manchester United, behind the scenes, the seeds of discontent were already being sown. Alex Ferguson began to see some of Beckham's 'extra-curricular' activities as damaging to his game. Becks had met the Spice Girl, Posh Spice, *at* United – she'd been there to perform the half-time entertainment – and they'd been in a relationship since 1997. In 1999, 'Posh and Becks' were married. It was a lavish affair, seemingly free of that special quality which is taste. One can't help but think what Sir Alex, the son of a shipbuilder in Glasgow, would have made of it all.

In fact, Fergie's views on the Beckhams' increasing media presence were actually made fairly plain. Sir Alex and Becks were to clash with depressing regularity over the next few years, and, though Becks helped United to their third Premier League title on the trot in 2000-01, Ferguson was increasingly quoted in the press, seemingly exasperated at his number 7's 'lifestyle'. To be fair to Beckham, these lifestyle concerns never truly affected his performance to the extent that they have, say, Wayne Rooney. But Ferguson likes to have absolute trust in his players, and if he senses their full attention is not invested in the job at hand, he loses that faith.

The Ferguson-Beckham relationship reached its nadir in 2003, with the 'Bootgate' incident. After an FA Cup defeat to Arsenal at Old Trafford, an angry Ferguson launched a boot in Beckham's direction. The boot hit Becks above the eye, leaving him requiring stitches. Then, much to Fergie's chagrin, Beckham chose to spend the next couple of days being 'papped' with the stitching above his eye very noticeable instead of keeping his head down and allowing the storm to blow over. And if there is one thing Sir Alex hated, it was things *not* being kept in-house at United.

Beckham was finally sold to Real Madrid in the summer of 2003. In his time at United, he'd brought joy to millions across the world. He'd walked with kings, but he'd never lost sight of that United touch. He won awards on and off the pitch. Captained England. Carried off six Premier League titles and an OBE, two FA Cups, and a Champions League. Alex Ferguson talks of Jaap Stam's leaving

121

the club being his one mistake in terms of taking a player as far as they can go, however, a case can be made for Beckham being another. After all, he's still playing now at the top level, and every time he's interviewed, he gets all misty-eyed about United.

Cristiano Ronaldo

Cristiano Ronaldo used to get misty-eyed quite a lot as a young player at the biggest club in the world, Manchester United. There were times he'd attempt a trick that wouldn't pay off, or he'd lose the ball, or he'd miss a chance, or some crude defender would smash him into the advertising hoards, and the cameras would home in on his face. You'd see his bottom lip trembling. Tears pricking his eyes. Sheer, childish frustration seeping out of his every pore. He resembled a good-looking version of Harry Enfield's teenager. As though he was about to moan, in Portuguese: *but it's just not FAIR.*

Now, of course, virtually every trick he tries pays off. Every chance he's presented with is buried in the back of the net. Every defender who confronts him is skinned, left on the seat of their pants; left, yes, with tears pricking the corners of their eyes. For Cristiano Ronaldo is nothing short of a beast of a footballer. He has all the attributes. He's tall and an excellent header of the ball. He's wonderfully skilful. He has an immensely powerful shot: his shots can dip and bend and swerve all at the same time. When Ronaldo hits a ball, the ball pitches and yaws, flies inexorably towards the target as though it is being piloted by a Soccer Starz figurine. He has an eye for a killer pass. He's strong. Built like a brick outhouse: he's said to undertake a staggering eight thousand sit-ups a day. Ronaldo is almost like a robot footballer. He's what a footballer would be like if he was invented, welded together from all the constituent parts. And like some feat of super-engineered weaponry, he has absolutely no mercy.

Watch him in a match. Watch the Darwinian processes his brain goes through as he tests each defender along the back-line for weaknesses, and then, in identifying the player he can *get at,* how he so mercilessly exploits it.

Unlike Messi, his perennial rival for the title of 'best player in the world', Ronaldo *looks* like a superhuman, bio-engineered athlete. The only reason we know he's *not* a fully fleshed-out robot is the fact we used to see him have his little tantrums when we first welcomed him onto English shores.

Cristiano Ronaldo dos Santos Aveiro – he was given the name 'Ronaldo' on account of his father's love of the American actor and president, Ronald Reagan – could so nearly have joined Arsenal. On these quirks of fate, history is made: the Madeiran made it as far as Arsenal's training ground in 2002, where he met with Arsène Wenger, however a contract was not offered to the player. Instead, Ronaldo returned to Sporting Lisbon, where, in a friendly to inaugurate the new stadium in 2003, he put in such a dazzling display that United's defenders returned to the dressing room with "twisted blood", and urged Fergie to sign up the right-winger who'd so tormented them immediately.

Fergie, of course, already knew all about Ronaldo. His extensive scouting network had already reported back on the winger, and Fergie liked what he heard. Indeed, part of the reason United agreed to take part in the friendly game in the first place was because Sir Alex wanted to cast his eye over the player. United paid just over £12m for Ronaldo a short time after the game, and Ferguson showed his faith in his new signing by presenting him with the fabled number 7 shirt so recently vacated by fans' favourite David Beckham.

Ronaldo's debut, against Bolton Wanderers, has now become the stuff of legend. In a half-hour cameo after coming on as a second-half substitute, the Portuguese showed the kind of skills United fans hadn't seen since another number 7: George Best. Yes: Ronny's debut was *that* good. And of course, we tried to temper our enthusiasm. We tried not to get too "Joey Barton" about it all – Barton had been the latest great blue hope at Manchester City, yet he was already showing signs he might not live up to the hype. But in the Trafford and the Tollgate, in Sam Platts and in pubs across Manchester, we couldn't hide our excitement at what we'd just witnessed.

Ronaldo had been all twists and turns, flicks and tricks. He'd danced around the Bolton defence time and again. He had played with an arrogance which belied his age. We loved him. And though there were inevitable dips in form during that first season – inevitable because he was still so young, so raw; inevitable because he was something of a mummy's boy living away from home for the first time – he still showed signs that he might grow into the player we all hoped he would, and not go all "Joey Barton" on us.

In fact, Ronaldo proved to be better than we'd even dared to dream. But more of that later. Initially we'll revisit Ronaldo's first honour in Red colours: the 2004 FA Cup. That year's final was held at Cardiff's Millennium Stadium due to reconstruction work at Wembley, and that day, our bedazzling number 7 played like a dragon. He breathed fire into a game which was seen as something of a *gimme* in some quarters – United were facing Millwall of the Championship – showcasing a new strength and intensity to his game which made him suddenly much harder to shake off the ball.

Suddenly Ronaldo was a beast. He'd been working on his physique all season and, when he scored the opener in United's eventual 3-0 triumph, he removed his shirt to show fans just how much work had actually been done behind the scenes. In contrast with that other shirtless celebration – Ryan Giggs' mad dash down the touchline after scoring the goal of the century against Arsenal in the FA Cup semi-final, twirling his shirt over his head and showing a majestic rainforest of chest hair – Ronny's exhibitionism showed him as a streamlined, sculpted, six-packed *monster.*

He looked like a statue of a Greek God: "Look on my works, ye Mighty," his body seemed to say, "and despair!"

Millwall did despair, and Ronaldo ran rampant. There was a moment deep into the second half which will always remain with me. Ronaldo had the ball close to the touch-line. He was confronted with the already exhausted Millwall full-back. Ronny performed a series of *at least twenty* step-overs. The full-back attempted to keep track; his head spun round and round as he followed the ball. He staggered. Tried to keep his feet. That "twisted blood" again.

Eventually, Ronaldo dinked it past him, and the dizzied full-back was so discombobulated he simply collapsed – like a Fred Dibnah-dynamited tower. Ronaldo, of course, received a standing ovation which lasted two minutes.

It was Ruud Van Nistelrooy, however, who scored the second and third goals, and carried off the sponsors' Man of the Match Award. United fans showed their (admittedly light-hearted) displeasure at this decision by roundly booing. Poor Van Nistelrooy mustn't have known what he'd done wrong. But it wasn't him, it was Him. Cristiano. The man for the big occasion. In his early years, a number of commentators criticized Ronaldo for a supposed inability to perform on the biggest stage, however United fans already knew different. Ronaldo *lived* for the big matches, the finals. He was also to score in his second final for the club, a season later, when United carried off the League Cup, having trounced Wigan Athletic 4-0, again at Cardiff.

And although United finished with only that League Cup as the sum total of their trophy haul in 2005-06, United fans were optimistic for the future, particularly as we appeared to have two of the most exciting young talents in world football plying their trade for us week-in, week-out. At face value, Wayne Rooney and Cristiano Ronaldo couldn't have appeared as more different. On the one hand we had the salt-of-the-earth Scouser Wayne, who looked, according to the wonderful, and sadly-missed, *The*

Guardian columnist Steven Wells "like a 45-year-old bouncer. One whose hobbies include stalking female newsreaders and whacking crucified kittens with a hammer." On the other, Cristiano, with his smouldering looks and his fancy-dan trickery and his gelled hair (Rooney, it seemed, had already been receding by the age of about ten).

Yet on the pitch, the two worked in glorious, devastating tandem, and had United fans salivating. We were desperate for the new season to start. We were sure the pair of them would just get better and better. We just had to get the 2006 World Cup out of the way and... Well, the 2006 World Cup in Germany *almost* put the kibosh on the dreams – those we'd dared dream about the Ron-Roo axis at any rate - before they'd even had a chance to get off the ground properly. You see, there was an ever so slight problem. Rooney's England were drawn against Ronny's Portugal in the quarter-final. Rooney, in a fit of frustration, was spotted stamping on Portugal and Chelsea defender Ricardo Carvalho. But what was *also* spotted was the sly, sneaky trickster Cristiano Ronaldo *winking* at the Portugal bench immediately after the red card was produced. At least, that was how the tabloid press would have us see it.

In Ronaldo, they had their Beckham Mark II, their ultimate villain, their man to blame for England's inevitable exit from the tournament – and note, there was very little recrimination for salt-of-the-earth Rooney, the man actually responsible for the stamp. No, swarthy Cristiano was to blame. Sneaky Cristiano must have told the Portugal players just how they could wind his United team-mate up, and *that* wink was him acknowledging the fact they'd got the job done.

According to the press, Rooney would ensure a warm welcome for Ronaldo upon his return to Manchester. According to the press, Ronaldo was already 'wimping out', looking for an alternative club abroad, somewhere he wouldn't have to face the backlash. In fact, there was some truth in this, but Ronaldo's move was not to come for another two years. Instead Rooney and Ronny quickly put the summer behind them and showed the tabloid press that the whole debacle had been nothing more than a storm in a German tea cup.

And Ronaldo, like Beckham before him, *used* the vitriol, the spite, the hatred which he suffered in his role as the nation's favourite villain. He had an absolutely barnstorming 2006–2007. He won

consecutive Player of the Month awards in
November and December. He *tore* into the
opposition at every opportunity. He took free-kicks.
We became accustomed to him standing over the
ball like a latterday Jonny Wilkinson, and then
screaming into a run-up, before smashing the dead
ball with such swerving, twisting power it was as
though he'd used some new and superhuman force.
He hit the ball like Neo dodged bullets in *The Matrix,*
like he personally controlled time and space.

United's number 7 was becoming more than
we'd ever dared dream he could be. He was playing
at a level far, far removed from his competitors: as
though he was an avatar in a football computer game
set to World Class when everyone else had to make
do with Amateur.

It was almost as though he was playing a
different sport.

In 2006-07, he broke the twenty-goal barrier
for the Reds from a wide-right position. In later
seasons for the Reds he'd drift inside, and hence his
record could be considered slightly skewed, but that
year, he was scoring bucket-loads as a winger. And
with Rooney also on the goal trail, United seized the
Premier League title back from Stamford Bridge in

some style. There'd been moments over the past couple of seasons, when United had made do with cup wins, when Mourinho's Chelsea had been steamrollering their way to league title after league title off the back of Roman Abramovich's billions, that we'd begun to worry that United might get left behind.

But in Ronaldo, we had a man light years *ahead* of everyone else.

Of course, he was substantially well-paid for his efforts. In 2007, he put pen to paper on a new contract which landed him a weekly £120k. He'd officially become the highest-paid player in the long and glorious history of the club.

But he was worth it.

The new contract had been granted in order to keep Ronaldo out of the jaws of the circling sharks of Real Madrid. And in the 2007-08 season, he was to reward the club's faith in him by delivering the second Champions League trophy of Sir Alex's United reign. Incredibly, that year the Portuguese's form eclipsed even that of the previous season. His goal-scoring record was phenomenal: he'd already equalled his 2006-07 goal haul by mid-January, and just kept going and going and going. A machine, he chalked up record after record: eventually, he'd walk away with Europe's 'Golden Boot' as the first ever winger to win the award But he was also popular amongst the players, and particularly with the manager. Indeed, Fergie made Ronaldo United captain for the first time in March 2008.

Ronaldo was, somewhat predictably, the scorer in the Champions League final of 2008, in Moscow. He leaped, as though off a spring-board, higher than the Chelsea defence to power home a header from a Wes Brown cross on the twenty-five minute mark prompting United fans to launch into the new song they'd debuted for the number 7 that season: *Viva Ronaldo*.

"Viva Ronaldo," went the song, "Viva Ronaldo. Running down the wing, hear United sing: Viva Ronaldo."

Not exactly original lyrics, but the fans didn't care. They sang it incessantly, drowning out their Chelsea counterparts, endeavouring to bellow the Champions League trophy off its perch and into United hands.

And yet Chelsea forced their way back into

the match. Frank Lampard scored a deflected equalizer and the match dragged on into a nail-biting extra-time period. And then, the dreaded penalties. Ronaldo, who'd heretofore showed an unerring accuracy and an unshakeable confidence from twelve-yards, was suddenly rocked by an attack of the jitters. Ronaldo's penalty-taking style had always incorporated a brief pause before he struck the ball. A *Matrix*-like moment in which he seemingly stopped time in order to ascertain which way the stopper was going to dive. In Moscow, however, Ronaldo paused for too long. You just knew he was going to miss. And he did. Thankfully, he was the only United player *not* to register his penalty on the night, and, thanks to John Terry's slip and Edwin van der Sar's eventual save from Nicolas Anelka's sudden death strike, United went on to lift the trophy.

But, as United fans celebrated exuberantly into the night, one man cut a forlorn figure on the Luzhniki Stadium turf. Cristiano Ronaldo lay prone in the centre circle, still inconsolable after his own, personal failure, despite the team's triumph.

And herein lies the rub with Ronaldo. He did seem overly concerned with his own performance.

His selfishness was so often decisive for United, but you sometimes got the impression he was achieving such amazing feats for 'CR7' as much as he was for MUFC. Contrast him with Wayne Rooney again. Consider the sheer number of occasions Roon was shunted out wide to 'put in a shift' for the side, as Sir Alex gave Ronaldo free reign to do what he wanted. Ronaldo didn't have to track back. Rooney spent some matches flitting between playing as a winger and a glorified full-back.

United reached another Champions League final in 2009, where this time we were to face Barcelona in Rome. Ronaldo, admittedly, had enjoyed yet another unbelievable season. He'd become the first Red since Georgie Best to win the Ballon d'Or. He passed the hundred mark in terms of goals scored for the club. Against a backdrop of shrill whistles and boos from the Porto crowd in recognition of his time at rivals Sporting Lisbon, Ronaldo took it upon himself to score what was surely the goal of his United career in the Champions League quarter-final, from some forty-five yards out. But at the Stadio Olimpico, Ronaldo was subdued. He tried *too* hard, just as he had with his stop-start penalty against Chelsea. One got the impression that he already knew it would be his final

135

game for United and was desperately trying to bow out on a (personal) high. Instead he disrupted the team performance. He consistently shot from long range, trying to replicate his Porto goal, but never came close. He only succeeded in giving the ball back to Barcelona.

And, as we all know, once you give Barcelona the ball, it is nigh on impossible to claim it back from them again. United went on to lose with something of a whimper. The game ended at 2-0, as did Ronaldo's career with the Red Devils. In June, Real's huge bid of £80 million was accepted by United's board. From what we've seen of Ronny in Spain, the "mob" Ferguson previously admitted he wouldn't even sell "a virus", had got our former number 7 for a steal. The boy's record in Spain has been like nothing football has ever seen before, apart from Lionel Messi, his eternal rival for the title of Best Player in the World.

When we first saw Ronaldo at the Theatre of Dreams, we'd hardly have dared dream of how high his stock would rise, but, in our more exuberant moments, maybe we might have whispered those words. The Best Player in the World. It is agonising to see him performing to such a consistently miraculous level for another side.

United fans have, over the past couple of seasons, began to sing a different version of the *Viva* song: "Viva Ronaldo, Viva Ronaldo. Put him on a plane, bring him back from Spain: Viva Ronaldo."

We sing it with a twinge of sadness in our hearts. But there's pride there too. Ronaldo is like some rare and beautiful creature we let go and we can still look at him and dream of when he was ours. In all, Ronaldo played 292 games for United, scoring 118 goals. Viva, forever.

Verdict: This is perhaps the toughest decision for any position in 'Team Fergie'.

Because David Beckham embodies all of those character traits of United-ness which won, for example, Patrice Evra his role in the ultimate side. And he's also got the supposed trump card of having come up through the ranks.

But Cristiano Ronaldo. Phew.

Though Cantona will - like Best, Charlton, Law and Edwards – continue to be the definitive darling of the United faithful, Ronaldo is simply the best player to have worn the United Red during Sir Alex Ferguson's time at Old Trafford. During his last couple of seasons at United, Ronaldo was simply *miles* better than anyone else plying their trade in the Premier League. He was so much better than everyone else, it was as though he was a different species. Though Beckham would win in the 'Top Red' stakes all day long, in this case, in playing terms alone, Ronaldo has to win.

Neil Custis waxes lyrical on the Portuguese maestro: "*Any* all time Manchester United team simply has to have Cristiano Ronaldo among the first names on the team sheet. That might prove controversial for some lifelong United fans who have seen a succession of greats at The Theatre of Dreams. But for me there has been nobody better that I have witnessed.

He was quite simply electric for United.

Sir Bobby Charlton himself once said Ronaldo was a player that drew you to the edge of your seat and it was a great analogy.

An incredible athlete; his speed, strength, skill and bravery destroyed teams. Yes bravery because this is a man who would be the victim of foul after foul but would get up and go again. His revenge would come with incredible goals. Witness that long ranger away at Porto or the header in Rome. The free kick against Portsmouth.

He is a player who changed games in the blink of an eye.

The only disappointment for me was his performance in the 2009 Champions League Final. It was the night he decided to have a personal duel with Lionel Messi and United suffered because of it.

You would love him to return, however, because that would make United a leading contender in Europe again."

7 - Central Midfield

Considering the fact this is Ferguson's Greatest United x11, the side will line up in classic Sir Alex style: four-four-two. Although Fergie revised this strategy in the latter years of his reign, particularly in Europe and in big Premier League clashes against rivals like Liverpool, Chelsea, Arsenal and Manchester City, preferring a more conservative line-up which was less likely to ship goals, when United are on song, at the top of their game, when the crowd are yelling *Attack, attack, attack-attack-attack!* it is this formation which really sets the pulse racing.

The two wingers flying, hammering in crosses for our two up front. The full-backs overlapping. Seemingly everyone in the side committed to going forward.

Which is why the anchoring midfielder is such a crucial vertebra in the spine of any Ferguson team. The anchoring midfielder plays a necessary role: they hold the team together when everyone else is pouring forward.

We're talking players like Roy Keane, Paul Ince, Owen Hargreaves, Michael Carrick, Darren Fletcher.

But which of these warriors have done enough to cement their place in Ferguson's Greatest x11? Which players have stood out?

Why don't we find out?

Roy Keane

I've often wondered what a magic hat might look like. Would it, for example, be a wizard's cone *a la* Mickey Mouse in *Fantasia,* or would it be a top hat, of the kind a magician can pull rabbits out of? Roy Keane, as the fans' song goes, wears a magic hat. *("Oh Keano's f***ing magic, he wears a magic hat, and when he saw Old Trafford, he said 'I fancy that. He didn't sign for Arsenal, or Blackburn 'cos they're s***e. He signed for Man United 'cos they're f***ing dynamite.")* Though I can't

141

imagine Keane deigning to wear either a magician's top hat or a wizard's cone. Not because he'd be embarrassed about how he looked in it, you understand, but on account of the fact Keane was never one for fripperies or foolishness of any sort.

That was for other players, at other clubs. Keane was for winning. And though he *did* perform a great number of magic tricks as a United player, and he succeeded in pulling any number of rabbits out of any number of hats - witness his dragging United back from the dead in our Champions League Semi-Final in Turin against Juventus in 1999 - he achieved these things through pure, unadulterated *will*.

Keane was drive and desire personified.

He was Keane.

He stripped back everything extraneous and became a soldier of will. If you are asked to bring an image of Keane to mind now, you likely won't imagine the younger Keane with his hair *dangerously close* to coming over his collar. You'll recall an older Keane. A Keane with his hair a step past crew-cut. His bald head gleamingly streamlined. The veins in his temples pumping with driven red blood. And

142

eyes burning with intensity. Nothing would get in his way. Hell, Roy Keane even walked his dog - poor old Triggs - as though he'd taken offence at the very ground he walked on. As though he wanted to pummel it into submission with his stomping feet.

Roy Keane was Keane. Keane to banish demons. Keane to win. Keane to drag United to another trophy, kicking and screaming if needs be.

Nothing magic about it. Just pure effort.

Roy Maurice Keane joined United in 1993 for a then British record transfer fee of £3.75 million from Nottingham Forest. At the time, there was some suggestion United had paid over the odds. *Four Four Two* magazine claimed Keane would need to win the European Cup single-handedly in order to pay back the hefty fee.

Funny that: fast-forward six years and that is almost exactly what Keane did, in the Semi-Final, at least.

United beat off strong competition from both Arsenal and Blackburn Rovers to attain his signature. Indeed, there were rumours Keane had already signed for Blackburn for £4 million, and only a personal phone call from Sir Alex – oh how those last-ditch phone calls, and out-of-the-blue house visits paid off for Fergie – made Keano change his mind. It wasn't only Sir Alex, however. Old Trafford, as the song suggested, played a large part in sealing the deal. Keane said I "fancy that." This was, of course, the start of a rather long and complicated relationship between the combative midfielder and United's stadium, and, at times, the fans. What's often forgotten about his infamous "prawn sandwiches" comments, which were aimed in the direction of the occasionally complacent home fans, was Keane's qualification: he always said United's hard-core, those who followed the team home and away, were the best in the world.

Early in his career, Keane had an eye for a goal. He scored twice on his debut, and followed that up with an unforgettable strike in the Manchester derby at Maine Road. That day, the City fans had mocked their United counterparts incessantly, reminding the Reds of their recent European Cup disaster at home to Galatasaray when, in a commanding position – 2-0 up – United had contrived to draw… In fact United had been lucky to even escape with a draw: only a late, late show from Eric Cantona rescued a point. But City were soon to have their jibes thrown back in their faces. They also took a 2-0 lead, only for United to drag themselves back into it. Only, unlike Galatasaray, United went on to win the match 3-2. "2-0 up and f***ed it up" indeed.

United won the double that year, and were in irrepressible form. The following year, however, brought the first signs of Keane's oft-discussed dark side. He saw red in the FA Cup Semi-Final replay at Villa Park against Crystal Palace, for stamping on Gareth Southgate. The original match had seen the tragic death of a Crystal Palace fan outside a Walsall pub, and the replay was *supposed* to be a more considerate affair. Clearly Keane hadn't read the script. His sending-off was the first of a sweep of eleven he achieved as a United player and there were rumblings in the media that Keane was not to be trusted.

Alex Ferguson, however, clearly didn't listen. He made Roy Keane his captain in 1997, after Cantona's departure, and the Cork-born star soon came to be seen as Ferguson's voice on the pitch. He was the very embodiment of Ferguson's own will to win... And his hatred of losing, and of complacency, and of settling for second best.

There was never any second best with Keane, nor with Ferguson. After all, to use a favoured Keane phrase: "Only dead fish go with the flow."

Keane went on to play a total of 480 games in a red shirt, scoring just over 50 goals. He won 7 Premier League titles, 4 FA Cups, 1 Champions League and 1 Intercontinental Cup. He is still adored by United fans. Reds will go all misty eyed as they remember his superhuman efforts for the cause. But he is also remembered for his dark side. The narrative of Keane's dark side was to continue throughout his career with the Old Trafford club. It saw its nadir in Keane's incredible revenge attack on Alf-Inge Håland in 2001, in the Manchester derby, recompense for a perceived insult earlier in Keane's career when he lay prone on the Elland Road turf in Leeds, and Håland loomed over him, accusing him of feigning injury. As if he would. And this dark side was increasingly seen during the latter stages of his United career as he seemingly raged against the - ever so slight - decline in his powers.

Suddenly Keane was lashing out, hurting those closest to him. Of course there was his "prawn sandwiches" comment, but Keane also struck out at his teammates over a supposed lack of effort on their part. And then, finally and decisively, Keane took on Ferguson himself. And there could only be one winner. Keane, formerly His Master's Voice on the pitch, the trusted lieutenant, was gone. Off to Celtic in the Scottish Premier League, where he won his last honour as a player, winning the league title.

Often, however, a player's impact can be measured by the size of the hole they leave behind in the team when they exit the club. Though all United fans knew what a crucial role Keane played in the side, and loved him for it, it was only in his absence we realised the immensity of the Trojan warrior we'd once had fighting on our side.

We'd been spoilt. We'd come to *expect* Keane's lion-hearted displays. In his twelve years at the club, we'd enjoyed unparalleled levels of success, and in so many crucial matches our captain had been the man carrying us through. Keane was the man picked up the trophies - he is still the United captain who has lifted the most FA Cups - but he was also the monster who drove the team forward. He was Ferguson's lieutenant on the field and woe betides anyone who didn't live up to his exacting standards.

147

Keane always had exacting standards. He expected maximum effort from himself - and from his colleagues - at every training session, let alone every match. Sometimes he couldn't understand why a player wasn't as Keane as him, or as driven. Dwight Yorke often refers to his first training session with United. Keane smashed a wild ball at him which Yorke failed to control. Then Keane gave him those murder-eyes. Growled: "Cantona would have killed that."

Keane could win a battle with his eyes. And he could win a football match before a ball was even kicked. Remember the tunnel at Highbury in 2005? Sky Sports cameras captured all of it, and you could almost smell the menace of Keane emanating from the screen as he stepped in to stop Patrick Vieira from intimidating Gary Neville. Keane was all prodding fingers and snarls, barbed insults and barely contained rage. In the match that followed, he continued to snarl, and bite and drive his team forward, translating his rage into complete domination of the midfield area. United went on to win 4-2, but the result was never in doubt from the moment our captain put Vieira well and truly in his place.

The Keane and Vieira tussles defined the mid-noughties, a period in which Manchester United and Arsenal were the two principal forces, and sparring partners, in English football. They had some monumental, heart-stirring battles.

Arsenal season ticket holder, Daniel Pearce, recalls the "epic battles" which took place between Vieira, "the immovable object" and Keane, "the irresistible force". Dan feels "rather dirty" for saying this, but: "Keane was someone who didn't hold back from any confrontation, whether on the pitch or off it. He was the player that left everything on the pitch and expected others to do the same. He was a leader. He had the capacity to lift his fellow players, the manager, the fans in the stands when it looked like things were going wrong. I think many opposition fans kind of overlook what an excellent footballer he was as well. I always got the sense that when Roy Keane played, to beat him and his team you had to play out of your skin, and when you defeated Manchester United then, the victory was even sweeter as you had well and truly earned it. A Roy Keane Manchester United never knew when it was beaten. Away to Juventus in 1999 was the perfect embodiment of that."

Ah yes, *that* Juventus match. Only, it wasn't a *match,* not really. More a locking of horns. The Juventus team of the mid-to-late 1990s were a real Keane-type team. They were tough, abrasive, and could run all day. They also boasted no little skill. They could outplay the opposition, but if it was a fight the other team wanted, then they could handle themselves that way too. This style had taken them to three Italian Championships in four years between 1994 and 1998 - including a double in 1994 - and they'd reached the last three Champions League finals. They'd also lost the previous two finals, and so were hell bent on winning the 1999 competition.

United drew the first leg in Manchester 1-1, with a late goal from Ryan Giggs at least giving them *some* hope for the second leg. But the Reds found themselves 2-0 down early in the game at the Stadio Delli Alpi. Even the most red-eyed of United fans must have suspected we were, yet again, going to exit the competition.

Enter Roy Keane. That night, Keano played with the single-minded determination of The Terminator, with a desperate rage burning inside him. He dragged the Red Devils back into the game with a header from a corner just before half-time - the ideal time to score. In the second half though, Keane was booked for a trip on Zinedine Zidane, which meant that he would miss the final. But Keane swiftly proved he was to be no Paul Gascoigne – there'd be no sobbing on the pitch for him - by leading the side to a dramatic 3-2 victory which, although sealed by goals from Cole and Yorke, had Roy Keane written all over it.

"Full steam ahead Barcelona," as Clive Tyldesley said, in commentary.

Sadly, there'd be no Barcelona for Keane. He and Paul Scholes were banned from the final. And after United's dramatic late victory, Keane was witnessed on the pitch in his suit. It was the one dampener on the magical occasion. Keane clearly felt out of place, celebrating the famous victory he'd had no part in. But what all United fans remembered was the fact there would have been no final at all, were it not for our indomitable number 16.

One last note on Roy Keane. We've discussed his 'dark side', and his Terminator-like will. We've discussed his outbursts and his indefatigability. We've mentioned the hard time he gave his poor dog Triggs whenever things went wrong. Because when they *did* go wrong – at times like when he stormed out of Ireland's 2002 World Cup preparations – he was always shown walking Triggs as though the poor dog was Dwight Yorke and he hadn't quite trapped a ball properly. Keane's testimonial was played at Old Trafford on 9 May 2006. United hosted Celtic. The crowd – sixty-nine and a half-thousand – is *still* the largest ever recorded for a testimonial match in England. And guess where all the proceeds went?

They went to Roy Maurice Keane - and his dog Triggs' - nominated charity: Guide Dogs for the Blind.

Paul Ince

If Paul Ince wore a hat, it was likely that hat would have been emblazoned with the legend 'The Guv'nor'. Certainly that was the name he had stitched into his matchday boots, and the one listed on his personalised numberplate. Incey was that type of guy.

The self-styled 'Guv'nor' was never lacking in confidence. Witness his posing in a United shirt before he'd even signed a contract with the Red Devils. This was an ill-advised act which only succeeded in embarrassing both clubs, and attracting the ire of the supporters who'd once loved him, during Ince's protracted transfer between the Uniteds of West Ham and Manchester in 1989. Indeed, Ince initially failed a medical, in August, before the move was finally put back on track in September of that year.

Ince joined for £1m, and it was immediately clear that it was money well-spent. He made his Red debut in a 5-1 win over Millwall at Old Trafford, although this was swiftly followed by a nightmare 5-1 defeat at the hands of Manchester City at Maine Road. But that was the kind of United side Ince had joined. They were horribly inconsistent: capable of lurching from the highest of highs to the lowest of lows from one week to the next. What they needed was someone strong enough to carry them through when the going got tough. Someone capable of raising their game, fighting for the cause. And Ince soon proved himself capable of rising to this challenge. Though United remained poor in the league – to such an extent that, in some sections of the support and in most of the media, there were calls for Fergie's head – they found their form in the FA Cup.

United had a remarkable run to the Cup Final in 1990. They were drawn away from home in every round, and had to visit some very tricky grounds, such as Forest's City Ground and Newcastle's St. James' Park. In the Semi-Final, they faced a plucky Oldham side which boasted a certain Denis Irwin at full-back, and, after a full-throttle first game which finished 3-3, the match went to a replay at Maine Road, which United won 2-1, with Mark Robins scoring the winner. The final too went to a replay after a 3-3 draw, United eventually seeing off Crystal Palace 1-0, thanks to a winner from Lee Martin (a full-back who Irwin would eventually replace). Ince was named man of the match in this game, which was some feat considering he'd been picked at right-back, in place of Viv Anderson.

The FA Cup win of 1990 was to prove the springboard for much of United's success over the next quarter of the century. For one thing, it secured Alex Ferguson's job as manager. For another, it gave young players such as Ince a new hunger for success and trophies. Ince swiftly became United's star midfielder. He was strong, tough in the tackle, and a driving force in the centre of the park. He revelled in the knowledge he was one of the leaders of the team. He was arrogant, certain of his own abilities, but for a team determined to put their stamp on English football, this was a good thing. It was the thing that would eventually help them to banish all of that uncertainty, all of that inconsistency, which had dogged them for the best part of twenty years. It would be the thing that would turn United from a renowned cup team into a proper challenger for the league title.

That league title would come in 1992-93: the inaugural season of the Premier League. Ince was in devastating form that year. He was clearly the best combative English midfielder, dominating his rivals up and down the country, particularly in the big matches against Liverpool, Arsenal, *et al.* But he was also showing a higher level of skill than fans had previously become accustomed to, and crucially, he'd added goals to his game.

Ince scored in the match which was to prove the coronation party – one massive, heaving sigh of relief after twenty-six years without a top division league trophy - a 3-1 victory against Blackburn

Rovers. Indeed, the United number 8 was to score in each of the last three matches of that fateful season.

But perhaps his most stand-out performance was on 5th April 1993 at Carrow Road, Norwich: a game Incey *didn't* score in. At the time, the inaugural Premier League was a three-horse race. United, Aston Villa, and, surprisingly, Norwich City were all in with a shout of the title. But Norwich were no flukes. This was an East Anglian side of rare confidence and ability, and they were to go on to have a dazzling run in the UEFA Cup the following season, in which they famously beat German giants Bayern Munich *in* Munich.

United went to Carrow Road on the back of a run of poor form. They'd contrived to lose at Oldham, before recording a hat-trick of draws against championship challengers Aston Villa, local rivals Manchester City, and George Graham's dour Arsenal. United had recorded just two goals in the four matches, and fans were starting to worry that *yet another* title collapse was on the cards.

But.

But United went to Carrow Road and played with a freedom, pace, and intensity which blew the

Canaries away. They were three goals to the good within twenty minutes, with goals from Giggs, Kanchelskis and Cantona. And every one of those goals was the result of a wonderful, sweeping move, with Paul Ince pulling the strings.

United were rampant that night. They were buccaneering. Marauding. They mercilessly put Norwich City to the sword, and the fans were jubilant. After that night, United won each and every one of their remaining games, and eventually won the league by a considerable margin.

But.

But that night at Carrow Road seemed to suggest to Paul Ince that he was more than a simple defensive midfielder, a breaker-up of play. It seemed to signal to him that he could now play with the freedom of some of the more attacking players in the side, like his great pal Ryan Giggs, or Eric Cantona.

Paul Ince, it seemed, began to believe his own hype.

Though he remained United's key midfielder for the 1993-94 season, behind the scenes, Fergie had lost his trust in the number 8. United lost out on the league that season, finishing an agonising second to Blackburn after failing to beat West Ham on the final day - a state of affairs which the Hammers fans took great delight in reminding Ince about. The Reds also lost in the FA Cup Final - 1-0 to Everton - and Ince was forced to shoulder some of the blame for the defeat. Ferguson felt that instead of tending to his defensive duties, Ince had expended too much energy marauding upfield, playing the hero role, the 'Guv'nor' role.

Worse was to come a year later, when Ince left for Internazionale of Milan in a £7.5 million move. After the move, Sir Alex didn't hold back in his criticism of the midfield general. He called Ince a "bottler" and a "big-time Charlie", referring to Ince's arrogance and his refusal to take instruction. The "Charlie" taunt was particularly damning. United fans regularly used it upon Ince's return to the Premier League, when he joined bitter rivals Liverpool. Then, there wasn't much love for Ince left, and fans' reaction to the player was as vitriolic as it had been for West Ham fans back in the day, but now we can look back on Ince's career, and the crucial roles he played in helping the club secure the first trophies of Alex Ferguson's reign. In his time at United, Ince won the Premier League and the FA

Cup twice. He also picked up medals in the
European Cup Winners' Cup and the League Cup.

Michael Carrick

Michael Carrick, Wallsend boy that he is, may well
have worn a coalminer's helmet had he been born
into a different decade. But if Roy Keane wore a
magic hat, and Paul Ince wore a cap with 'Guv'nor'
on it, then Michael Carrick wears an entirely
different form of headwear on the football field. He
wears green eyeshades: the type of visor commonly
worn by accountants, or similar, whose work with
the small details, under harsh halogen lights, can
prove a strain to the eyes after a while. Because
Michael Carrick has an accountants' zeal for the
details of a football match. He pulls strings, searches
for – often miniscule – gaps. And, when the
opportunity presents itself, he plays a killer ball.

Carrick plays the percentages. He weighs up
the options like a mathematician. And like an
accountant, he is miserly. If humanly possible,

159

Carrick wouldn't allow the opponents a single touch of the ball. It is as though he'll be heavily taxed for giving the ball away.

Of course, none of this sounds as exciting as the lung-busting midfield runs of a Paul Ince, or the heroic drive and will to win of a Roy Keane, and, during his time at United, Carrick has been very much the unsung hero because of the often quiet and unassuming way in which he runs his matches. It took Carrick *seven years* at United before he was rewarded with a song for his efforts – more on that later. And indeed, over the years, the boy from the north east has been treated with some scepticism by fans, some of whom liked to compare him to Ray 'The Crab' Wilkins on account of his penchant for passing the ball sideways, always sideways.

On closer examination though, it must be said that Carrick is, in fact, an excellent passer of the ball. His range of passing is second to none in the Premier League at the moment: he can pull off the Hoddle-style long pass, or the Scholes-a-like quarterback pass, or the Sheringham-esque through-ball. Crucially, he *keeps* the ball. He's a miser when it comes to allowing the opposition a touch, and even when they are in possession, Carrick isn't the type of

160

central midfielder we're used to because he hardly ever tackles. He doesn't go charging in, risking yellow and red cards. United fans have never seen him clatter an opponent. Doesn't need to. Much like Rio Ferdinand, he reads the game too well for that.

And yet, when Michael Carrick was nominated for the PFA Player of the Year award for his sterling work in the 2012-13 season, the likes *Talk Sport* ran numerous phone-ins in which football fans from all over the country called to vent their spleen. Not many could understand why Carrick deserved the nod. Even some Reds were left scratching their heads.

Mind you, Michael Carrick has *always* been up against it at United. He arrived in 2006, thanklessly tasked with filling the Grand Canyon-sized gap left by one Roy Maurice Keane. And he arrived with a hefty price tag too: Tottenham's Daniel Levy driving up the transfer fee to an extortionate-seeming £14 million (rising to £18.6 million when certain appearance clauses were triggered). Carrick, soft-spoken as he is, wasn't one to shirk a challenge, however. He was offered his pick of shirt numbers at United, and it was *his choice* to wear the number 16 shirt vacated by Keane.

Carrick was schooled at West Ham's 'Academy'. In 1999, when Manchester United were sweeping all before them to secure a unique treble, Carrick (and his then side-kick Joe Cole, who Carrick would later line up against in the 2008 Champions League Final against Chelsea in Moscow) was helping West Ham's youth team conquer all before them in that year's FA Youth Cup. They won the final by a record aggregate score of 9-0 against Coventry City.

After breaking through to the West Ham first team, Carrick enjoyed a couple of strong seasons, though he also faced the heartbreak of relegation. He played one season in the Championship before declaring he needed to play Premier League football. Tottenham Hotspur stepped in, and Carrick enjoyed two seasons at White Hart Lane, making something of a name for himself as an elegant, cultured midfielder with an eye for a killer pass. Soon his form attracted the attention of Sir Alex Ferguson, and the rest was history.

There were some notable moments in Carrick's first season as a Red, a season which would conclude with United carrying off another Premier

League title. His headline performance though, came in the Champions League. United had been handed a tough draw in the quarter-final, facing the Italian giants Roma. And in a first leg at Rome's Coliseum of football, the Stadio Olimpico which was marred by off-pitch incidents – the heavy-handed Italian police waded in to the away stand and hit out at defenceless fans with batons and there were numerous reports of stabbings outside the ground – United had fallen to a 2-1 defeat. This blow was doubled by the fact our star midfielder, Paul Scholes, was sent off, and was thus banned for the second leg.

Tensions were riding high on a balmy April night as the two teams prepared to take the field for the second leg. There was also an air of nervousness amongst the crowd. Reds wondered whether – without Scholes – we'd be able to deal with Roma's classy midfield, which boasted the combative Daniele De Rossi, and the genius of the deep-lying forward, Francesco Totti. And these worries were not exactly assuaged when the news of Ferguson's team selection reached us. For it seemed the key area at the centre of the park would be comprised of the disappointing striker-who-never-scored Alan Smith, and Michael Carrick: a fine passer of the ball, but hardly a man you could trust to put his foot in. And surely this was a night we *needed* a player who could put his foot in.

We couldn't have been proved more wrong. Yet again, Fergie *knew*. He knew where and how we could get at Roma, and, instead of worrying about the opposition and how they could hurt us, he set out his United side in order that we could hurt them. And how. Carrick was a giant that night. His head was up, constantly tick-tocking from side to side. He spotted gaps, he sprayed passes. He pulled strings. He also scored goals: two, on a famous night in which United ran out 7 (seven) – 1 winners.

Sadly, United went on to lose the semi-final, in which we were again drawn against Italian opposition. An aging AC Milan team put us out, 5-3 on aggregate. Even worse, Milan went on to play Liverpool in the final. And we all know what happened there.

And yet, after all this, Michael Carrick started the 2007-08 season without a guarantee of a place in the first team. Fergie, ever hungry to freshen up the squad, had brought in the England midfielder Owen Hargreaves, from Bayern Munich. Anderson had also joined, from Porto. Both came with hefty price tags attached. Injury too robbed him of playing time during the early months of the season. But it was in the second half of the season that Carrick truly came to the fore as a United player. His excellent form drove United on to win the Premier League trophy again, at the expense of Chelsea.

And it was Chelsea who stood between United and their second Champions League trophy in the Ferguson era. The final was held in Moscow on 21st May, and was as tightly contested as the Premier League title race had been. United dominated the first half and were rewarded with a Ronaldo header which gave them the lead. But Chelsea pegged United back with a Frank Lampard goal on the stroke of half-time, and in the second half, began to take over. Eventually, the game went into Extra-Time, and then finally, to penalty kicks.

Carrick played the full 120 minutes, and took, and scored, one of the spot-kicks which helped United to win the trophy.

In subsequent seasons, it was Carrick's form in United's *other* Champions League finals of the Ferguson era which seemed to define supporters' opinion of him. He remained at his elegant best in the Premier League, but when he was forced to

165

make that step up, to compete against players of the highest level, he was found wanting. In 2009, United reached their second Champions League final in a row. They faced Barcelona in Rome, the site of those ugly scenes back in 2007. On the night, United simply couldn't live with the Catalan giants. The midfield in particular were completely over-run, out-passed, and out-schemed by their Barcelona counterparts.

In 2011, United were offered a chance at redemption against the same opponents. This time the final was to be held at Wembley, scene of United's first European Cup triumph, back in 1968. But Barcelona too had an affinity with Wembley, having won their own first European Cup under the shadow of the twin towers. And by 2011, Barcelona were unquestionably the best club side in Europe. Their players were devastatingly high on confidence: most of them were World Cup and European Championships winners with Spain, and in one of the ones who wasn't – Lionel Messi – they had the best player in the world.

The game was to follow a similar script to Rome. Barcelona were simply too good for United, as they'd have been too good for *anyone* who'd lined up against them on the night. And though Rooney offered United fans some hope with a 34th minute equaliser after Pedro had given Barcelona the lead, the Catalans simply swatted United aside in the second half: Messi and Villa registered strikes for Barca and, in truth, it could have been more than three. Again the midfield had been bossed, again Michael Carrick had failed his audition at the highest level.

However, we shouldn't hold this against him. Forget Messi for a moment: in Rome and at Wembley, Carrick was faced with perhaps the best midfield ever assembled at club level in Europe. And who knows how Roy Keane, or Paul Ince, would have coped against such luminaries as Xavi and Andrés Iniesta. Perhaps Carrick, and that United side in general, were simply unlucky. Unlucky to be the undoubted *second best* in Europe at a time when the greatest club side ever were in their pomp. Of course, Roy Keane wouldn't have accepted second best, but the question remains as to how he would have coped with such sustained and skilled examinations at the hands of Barcelona's stars.

Lest it be forgotten, Michael Carrick has now enjoyed six seasons at United, and he's played over

167

three hundred games for the Reds. And over this period, we've enjoyed a great deal of success. And finally, six seasons in to his Red career, United was finally recognised by fans with a song, all of his very own.

Here's how it goes (to the music of *Magic,* by Pilot):

"Woah-oh-oh, it's Carrick, you know. Hard to believe it's not Scholes. Carrick, you know."

United fans *do* know, even if everyone else in the football world doesn't. It's Carrick, you know. Maybe he *is* fit to lace Roy Keane's boots. Maybe he can fill that number 16 shirt.

And maybe when he leaves, there'll be a Carrick-shaped hole to fill.

Verdict: Over the years some true greats have graced United's midfield.

But, like *Highlander,* there can be only one represented here. And though there are some doubts over Roy Keane's temperament, as well as our over-reliance on our broad-shouldered number 16 – my dad, a veritable encyclopaedia on all things United and the most rabid fan I've ever met, sounds this note of caution: "the issue I had with Keane was he so dominated the team that when he was (frequently) injured towards the end, we were regularly rudderless" – Keane's performances, his drive, and his domination were actually what made us all love him so much.

And even if you didn't love him, if you were, say, a fan of one of our bitterest rivals, then you *respected* him. This is Arsenal season-ticket holder, Daniel Pearce on Keane: "Fergie has pulled together some outstanding teams in his time as United manager, but the treble winning side for me was the best bar none. For a team to be so good, and yet Keane to lead it and stand out in it is some feat."

Indeed, some Reds fans argue that there is *still* a stand-out, Roy Keane-sized, hole in the middle of the park some eight years after Keano left, in 2005. And Sir Alex knew that Keane would be absolutely impossible to replace, so he didn't even try. Instead he signed a different type of midfielder, in Michael Carrick. Ferguson has not signed a central midfielder since he brought in Hargreaves in 2007 – the youngster Nick Powell's arrival, and Scholes'

169

dramatic retirement u-turn notwithstanding – so perhaps he too knows that nothing compares to Roy.

Neil Custis says: "Keane was simply the engine in the greatest ever period in United's history.

They would not have achieved anything like they did without him. He made United tick. If a player was in trouble Keane was always the player there to help. Constantly available, constantly in control of games, an incredible player."

Sir Alex, when asked to describe what he felt was key to a "winning mentality" named two things. "A will to win. And attention to detail." Most players embodied one of those aspects (such as Carrick and his fastidious play). But it takes a rare player, such as Keane, and his almost obsessive compulsive desire for proper preparation (to prevent p**s poor performance) as witnessed in his Ireland World Cup walk-out, when allied with his murderous drive to win, almost at all costs, who embodies both.

8 - Central Midfield

Alongside our midfield 'anchor' the 'Team Fergie' boat needs an engine. One that can travel at a rate of knots from box to box, providing the kind of action-packed displays the Old Trafford crowd *yearn* for as the team grind through the gears on attack after attack. Manchester United have had a wide and varied range of central midfielders who act as the heartbeat in the engine-room of the side.

We've seen the sleek, purring type. We've seen the full-throttle, high-octane type. We've seen brave skippers; hearty crewmen. We've seen showy speedboats: those who've come with big money price-tags; and flagships: those who've progressed through the ranks of the youth team before exploding onto the scene, filling us with pride. We've seen rudders: players who dictate the direction and forward momentum of the side.

In the final analysis however, there are two *types* that stand-out here: the box-to-box midfielder, and the wily scheming midfielder. For each of those

171

types, we'll look at the one stand-out performer, and consider their merits.

Bryan Robson

When asked to name the best central midfielder under Sir Alex Ferguson, Norman Whiteside was definitive in his answer. "Bryan Robson, without a doubt," the Northern Irishman said. "Robbo was, no question, the best midfield player of his generation." Big Norm should know, having played alongside Robbo when the player was at the height of his powers.

And they were some powers. Bryan Robson at his peak was like a comic book hero. He was like Roy of the Rovers, Superman, and Indiana Jones all rolled into one. He was the original 'Captain Marvel'. To paraphrase the fans' song, there was only one Bryan Robson.

Fans loved our one-of-a-kind central-midfielder. During the dark days of the apocalyptic final months of the Ron Atkinson era and the fragile early years of the Ferguson dynasty, he was United's one guiding light, our one *gen-yoo-ine* superstar, our one bonafide world-class talent. He was our protective shield; the reminder of the club's greatness. Sure we were rubbish, *mostly,* but we had Robbo.

On one of my earliest trips to Wembley – for the League Cup final in 1992 – I remember sitting in the cheap seats which advertised a 'restricted view'. This turned out to be a massive great pillar right in the way of the pitch, and, if you somehow cranked your head to look round that, a huge fence (to keep the fans in). As there wasn't much to see on the pitch, I stood and watched the fans around me. Many of them were very, very drunk: the perennial Wembley sun having *baked* the drunkenness into them. One particular guy was lying across about five seats, clearly incapacitated. Couldn't even open his eyes. But when a policeman entered the scene and asked him to move, he launched into action.

"Will you move please, sir?" (The sir through gritted teeth.)

The drunk allowed a tiny smile to play at the corners of his lips. He held a single finger aloft.

Began to sing: "There's only one Bryan Robson."

No matter what the policeman said, this was the drunk's answer. One Robson. Over and over again like it was his shield, his get out of jail free card, his silver lining. It was the drunk's answer for everything, and Robson was the answer for everything for that United team. He was the be all and end all. The One and Only. And what was truly amazing was the fact *Robbo wasn't even playing* that day.

Bryan Robson was the longest-serving captain in the long and proud history of Manchester United. The Chester-le-Street born star skippered the Reds to a trio of FA Cups, as well as a European Cup Winners' Cup crown and, as his career waned, he finally added two Premier League titles to his roll call of honours. As well as being a firm fans' favourite – particularly amongst those who lived through the aforementioned 'dark days' – he was also immensely popular amongst his fellow players. Indeed, in an August 2011 poll of ex-United players to mark the securing of United's nineteenth championship, Robbo was voted the Red Devils' greatest ever player, and both Bobby Robson and Tony Adams named him in their respective 'dream teams'.

Captain Marvel made his debut for West Bromwich Albion at humble York City way back in April 1975. On the same day in history, the US evacuated their embassy in Cambodia. There was long hair and flared trousers on the terraces, and even a cursory glance at the Panini sticker albums of the day show you that the same styles were favoured by a lot of the players: Robbo himself was to sport a white 'Afro' during his West Brom days. But he never evacuated *anywhere*.

Especially not a pub.

Robbo impressed in his debut season, but in the following season the boy from the north east struggled to nail down a permanent place in the side. It didn't help that West Brom's new player-manager was one (ex-Red) Johnny Giles, who just so happened to prefer Robbo's central-midfield berth. Still, the Baggies were promoted in 1975-76 and Robson began to stake a claim for a more regular starting-role with some stand-out performances in the top flight. That season, however, in addition to showing the first signs that he might be a Superman, Robbo also showed us his kryptonite.

He broke his leg, and his right ankle that year.

175

Then Albion appointed a new manager: Ron Atkinson. And though Big Ron did have some initial misgivings about Robbo, these were soon set aside in 1978-79, when he made Robson the fulcrum of the side – and the number 7 – as the Baggies flew to third in Division One and reached the quarter-final of the UEFA Cup. And when Atkinson left for United in 1981, Robbo joined shortly afterwards for a British record transfer fee of £1.5 million. As befitting United's new Great White Hope, he signed amidst much razamatazz *on the pitch* before a game on 1st October 1981: a moment of pure theatre at the Theatre of Dreams. He would make his Red debut less than a week later, at Spurs in the League Cup.

In 1983, however, his kryptonite showed up all over again: Robson tore ankle ligaments in the League Cup semi-final against Arsenal, and missed the final in which United lost against Liverpool. He regained his fitness in time for the FA Cup semi-final though, and found the net in a victory (again against Arsenal). And this time he made the final too, in which he scored a brace (and could have had a hat-trick had he not selflessly allowed Arnold Muhren to take a penalty in the 4-0 replay thrashing).

And Robson donned his Superman cloak again in the next season's European Cup Winners' Cup. Fans of a certain age still hark back to the frenzied, pulsating atmosphere of that famous European night at Old Trafford – they say it's the best they ever experienced – in which a Robson-inspired United fought back from a 2-0 first leg deficit to win the second leg 3-0. Robbo scored twice that night, keeping up his useful habit of scoring in the big United matches, and United looked on course to pick up their first European silverware since 1968, but our Captain Marvel's injury problems again resurfaced, and he was forced to sit out both legs of the semi-final against Juventus, and the Italian club ultimately triumphed. They went on to win the final too, beating Porto 2-1 in Basel.

Robbo lifted another FA Cup in 1985 after another captain's performance in the Wembley final against champions Everton. Big Norman Whiteside scored a fantastic winner in extra-time after United had been reduced to ten men – Kevin Moran becoming the first player to be sent off in an FA Cup final. And the signs were looking good for a crack at the league title the following year, especially as they won the first ten straight league matches of

177

the 1985-86 season. However, transfer speculation regarding United's young Welsh tyro, Mark Hughes, and *another* Robson injury – this time a dislocated shoulder - meant that although United started like a train, they ended the season derailed.

Ron Atkinson's United never recovered from the disappointment of tailing off so badly in the 1985-86 season. Indeed, by November of the following season, Atkinson was gone, replaced by the Scot Alex Ferguson, who'd had a successful spell up at Aberdeen where he'd challenged the Old Firm hegemony. At Old Trafford, Fergie's mission would be even more trying: he was faced with knocking a hugely successful Liverpool side off their "perch". But Fergie's problems when he arrived at United weren't only external. He was also faced with an Old Trafford which was stricken with internal problems and strife.

There were rumours of an incorrigible drinking culture within the Red ranks and Fergie's first great test, before he could even think of taking on Liverpool, was to break up that team within a team – United's drinking team. With this in mind, Fergie soon got rid of Paul McGrath and Norman Whiteside, but Bryan Robson, another member of that team, was deemed simply too good to let go. As well as being a superhuman player, Robbo, it was said, possessed superhuman powers of recovery. He could smash even the worst hangovers into submission and stand up and play like a lion the next day. One can only wonder, however, how many injuries Captain Marvel might have avoided if he had prepared for matches the way players do today.

The rebuilding of the team under Fergie was painfully slow. Too slow for some fans, who called for Sir Alex's head in 1990 when the Reds were yet again struggling to find decent form in the league. It was the FA Cup that saved him, and again, Robbo played a crucial role in the delivery of "Old Big Ears" to the Theatre of Dreams. He was to continue his habit of scoring in finals and semi-finals, with a goal in the semi-final 3-3 draw against Oldham at Maine Road, and another in the Wembley final, which again ended 3-3 (before United went on to edge the replay 1-0). In winning the cup, Robbo became the first captain to lift a hat-trick of FA Cups.

But injury reared its ugly head yet again in 1990-91. Robbo was injured in the World Cup in Italy, and was out for more than half of the season:

the first time he pulled on a Red shirt that season
was in December. But he was back in time for the
run to the European Cup Winners' Cup final, in
which United went two stages further than they had
in 1984, and reached the final, in Rotterdam, where
two goals from Mark Hughes secured the trophy.

In 1991-92, Uniteds prospects in the league
continued to improve – they were to narrowly miss
out on the title: pipped at the post by Leeds – but
Robbo's seasons in the sun for the Reds continued
to be curtailed by injury. He was to miss the League
Cup final win against Nottingham Forest that year
and even when fit, was facing increased competition
for a midfield role from young pretenders such as
Paul Ince. Then, in 1992-93, United finally won the
league championship, but Robbo was far from being
the first-choice midfielder. Ince, Mike Phelan, and
the converted forward Brian McClair, were now
higher up the pecking order than Captain Marvel.
And a further indication of Robbo's reduced role
was provided when, for the first time, squad
numbers were issued for the new Premier League
season of 1993-94 and Robson was given the
number 12 jersey instead of his famous number 7
(which went to Eric Cantona). Robbo still played
enough games to qualify for a championship

winner's medal, but the vast majority of them were as a substitute.

He was still a bonafide FA Cup hero though. The very last of his 99 goals in club colours came in the 1993-94 semi-final (again against Oldham, again in a replay, again at Maine Road). Sadly though, Fergie dropped Robson from his FA Cup final squad, and Robbo's last appearance came on the final day of the league season, in the dead-rubber league game against Coventry, which finished as a 0-0 draw.

Over the years a lot of players have been dubbed the 'next Bryan Robson'. Interestingly, one of the comparisons most often drawn is between Robbo and Steven Gerrard, over at bitter rivals Liverpool. But to most observers, Robson was the original and best. If you never saw Robbo play, you were unlucky. He was Steven Gerrard with the positional-sense section of the brain fully-wired; Gerrard without the selfish Hollywood balls every five minutes; Gerrard without the e numbers; Gerrard who hadn't read too much Roy of the Rovers, who didn't think the script of every match had to have him as the star. Robbo was Gerrard *plus-one*.

Stevie Gerrard often appears to play for himself, for his own personal glory, first. With Robson, it was always about the team, almost to the detriment of his own game: witness his sheer number of injuries when he put his body and soul on the line. Robson wasn't afraid of letting others take the glory. He just wanted to win.

After United, Robbo moved to Middlesbrough, where he was made player-manager. His final appearance as a player came in January 1997 (on New Year's Day) when the nearly 40 year-old, showing no signs of a hangover, took the field against Arsenal at Highbury.

In March 2011, Robson revealed he'd had surgery for throat cancer, but, a winner to the last, Captain Marvel saw off that threat and lived on to fight another day.

Paul Scholes

The ginger prince, Paul Scholes, is something of an enigma. Although he is capable of the most incredible feats on a football field, and he's not scared of performing the most outrageous tricks in front of 76,000 spectators, he's also one of the shyest people you might ever encounter. On the rare occasions he's caught by an interviewer, he speaks quietly into his chest. His eyes resemble those of a rabbit caught in the headlights. His stance says everything about how he can't wait to simply high-tail it out of there at the earliest possible opportunity.

Another thing: the man who has been, undoubtedly the most elegant, graceful, and artistic English-born player in decades, the man who can do things with a football that only Zinedine Zidane could match – *Mona Lisa* passes, Picasso volleys, Monet wonder goals - is also capable of launching into the crudest, most agricultural challenges on his fellow professionals this side of Vinny Jones.

Paul Scholes is a man of contrasts. He's wildly *normal.* Just a Salford-born, Middleton-raised

183

lad playing for his local team. And yet at the same time, had he been born on the streets of Buenos Aires or Rio, he'd have been talked of as one of the most cultured players of his generation. He's a relative failure at international level (though through no fault of his own – all too often he was under-appreciated and played out of position) and yet, in Champions League circles, he's still talked of as one of the best. He's like a footballer from a bygone era – witness his dogged one-club nature, and the way he has about him which suggests he'd quite happily travel to matches on the bus, with fans, as long as he didn't have to chat to them much – and yet he's like a player from the future too: his style, his grace, his regal-bearing, the way he dissects a football pitch so mathematically-precisely suggesting a new type of midfielder.

He's incredibly unselfish, happy for his team-mates to hog the glory. And yet, he's as protective of the ball as the kid who won't share his toy with anyone else. His ball-retention skills, his excellent passing abilities, his long shooting attributes, his capacity to score wonder goals – he's the player who was given just about everything (except tackling) and yet you get the impression he's worked hard to get where he is too. Made   his own luck.

He's missed a huge number of matches through his poor disciplinary record: Scholesy's been sent off ten times and booked 120 times in all competitions. He's the third most-booked player in Premier League history, and his 32 yellow cards in the Champions League make him the head-and-shoulders leader in terms of bookings in that competition. And yet, despite all the suspensions, he's amassed over 700 appearances for United, giving him the third-highest number of appearances for the Reds in history.

He's the man who has won pretty much everything in the game – a read-it-and-weep eleven Premier League titles, two Champions Leagues, three FA Cups, and two League Cups – and yet you get the feeling that, instead of going out and partying hard with his team-mates, he'd like to do nothing more to celebrate than sit with his feet up in front of the telly, or else go and watch his beloved Oldham Athletic with his mini-me kids.

He's the man who came up through the ranks with David Beckham, of all people. And indeed, Scholesy is like the *anti*-Becks. He's Becks without any of the frills and the celebrity. You get the impression that the most 'celebrity' Scholesy would get is in adding an extra sugar to his cuppa.

Paul Scholes began training with United at the tender age of 14. Though too young for the 'Class of '92' FA Youth cup-winning side which contained the likes of Beckham, Gary Neville, Nicky Butt and Ryan Giggs, he played in the slightly less famous side which made it all the way to the final the following season, alongside Phil Neville. It was still an incredible harvest for Eric Harrison and the rest of the youth team coaches, and one which we may never see the like of again.

It took some time for Scholesy to progress to the first team. And while Giggsy *et al* were helping United secure the club's first league championship for 26 years in 1992-93, there was still some doubt as to whether Paul would make it. There were issues with his asthma, and with the fact that Scholes was nominally a striker, and there wasn't exactly much room for another striker in the first-team squad at the time. However, in spite of the odds, by 1994-95, Scholesy had put himself in contention and, finally took his bow for the first team in that perennial trial-ground for the big time which is the League Cup. His debut came at Vale Park, Port Vale on 21st September. When the team-sheets were announced, the Port Vale chairman was forthright in his criticism of United's policy of blooding youngsters in the cup, thus depriving the Vale Park faithful of seeing players of the ilk of Roy Keane and Eric Cantona. Of course, given the benefit of hindsight, he couldn't have looked more foolish. For the United side that took the field that game was star-studded. Scholes, Beckham, Butt, the Nevilles. Between them they'd go on to win huge numbers of England caps and would become one of the most decorated groups of players ever to play football in England. Scholes scored both goals against Port Vale and went on to be picked for his Premier League debut less than a week later, in a poor-showing at Portman Road against Ipswich, when United lost 3-2. Scholes registered a goal in this match too.

But he was still very much a squad player. His big break was to come in 1995-96, when Fergie famously gave youth its chance and Alan Hansen made even more of a fool of himself than the Port Vale chairman when he made that notorious remark about nobody winning anything "with kids". Scholes was upgraded from the number 24 shirt to the number 22 shirt for the season and, without Mark Hughes standing in his way, he had the run of matches he'd sorely needed, weighing in with 14 goals in all competitions, and eventually picking up a Premier League winner's medal and an FA Cup winner's medal, after Cantona's goal downed Liverpool in the FA Cup final.

In 1996-97, Scholesy upgraded again, changing his shirt number to the famous number 18, which he was to wear for the next fifteen years. But in 1997-98 came his most famous upgrade, when he shifted back from the floating 'number 10' role into his now preferred central-midfield berth in the wake of Roy Keane's knee injury suffered at Elland Road. United missed out on silverware that season, but in the following season, United, with Scholes at the hub of everything, flourished into one of the best club sides ever seen in the English game. And although Scholes missed the crowning moment of the 1998-99 season – he was banned from the Champions League final in Barcelona through suspension – he was able to deliver one of the crucial aspects of our treble, by scoring one of the goals in the FA Cup final at Wembley against Newcastle.

In 2001-02, Fergie tried to upgrade the whole United midfield. United boasted arguably

Europe's best midfield at the time (with Beckham, Keane, Scholes and Giggs all at their pomp) however Ferguson has always known that in order for a team to remain successful, and to avoid resting on its laurels, it must be constantly refreshed, improved, given new challenges. He brought in the costly Juan Sebastian Veron, from Serie A. And much as Veron was a wonderful player, his signature seemed to disrupt the flow of the team. It brought about a change in formation, to United's now familiar 4-4-1-1. Scholes' form in particular suffered.

But the following season, he was back with a vengeance, scoring a career-high twenty goals in all competitions.

A low point came in 2005, in the FA Cup final in Cardiff, when United, undoubtedly the best team over 120 pulsating minutes, were taken to penalties by a dogged Arsenal. Scholes missed his penalty and Arsenal went on to win a rather undeserved trophy. History has a way of paying these things back though – that trophy remains the last Arsenal have added to their cabinet in all the intervening years.

2006 brought up Scholesy's five-hundredth match in United colours. But in 2008 he finally made up for one of the crucial matches he'd sadly missed over his previous 14 years at the club. United reached the Champions League final again, and with his suspension from the 1999 final in Barcelona in mind, Fergie announced Scholes would be the first name on his team-sheet for the '08 final against Chelsea in Moscow. He'd also played a major part in securing United's safe passage to the final, with the match-winner against Barcelona in the semi-final at Old Trafford: a customary, devastating Scholes blockbuster from outside the box. In the final, Scholes performed well, but, after a late 50/50 with the Chelsea anchor Claude Makelele, he received a yellow card and was also taken off, injured. He wouldn't play any role in the extra time, or in the penalty shoot-out. Still, when United won, he at least had a Champions League medal he could feel proud of.

That yellow card though. We discussed earlier the sheer number of red and yellow cards Scholes amassed. And as his career entered its twilight years, as he lost a yard of pace, it seemed as though the ginger prince was booked every single match. Indeed, some United wags joked that the referee might as well issue Scholesy with a yellow card as the teams entered the field of play, just to get his customary booking over and done with.

He was amassing other records though too. Moving further and further back on the field allowed him to take up a 'quarterback' role which he excelled in. It allowed him to *use* his full array of passes, to stimulate attacks from deeper. To hold the ball longer. In 2009, he made his 600th appearance for United, against Portsmouth. And he wasn't just a 'sympathy pick' for Fergie, during 2010 and 2011. (I don't think anyone truly thinks Sir Alex has *ever* picked a player based purely on sympathy, except maybe Ole Gunnar Solksjaer right at the end, when injury had ravaged him.) But in 2011, Scholes himself began to feel the dying of his own light, much as Gary Neville had done. He began to believe he was costing the team. In particular, he felt his daft sending-off in the FA Cup semi-final against "noisy neighbours" Manchester City - who were newly flush with petro-dollars – had contributed to United's 1-0 defeat. Something which allowed City to win their first trophy in most people's lifetime. Of course, on the same day City won their FA Cup, United trumped them by winning the Premier League, but still. One rash tackle from Scholesy, and City were on the trophy trail…

With this in mind, Paul Scholes retired from football on 31st May 2011. A testimonial was played, against New York Cosmos, at Old Trafford. It was all over. The fat lady had sung. She was now in her dressing room, removing her make-up. Scholes was gone. We would never see his like again.

Or would we?

In January 2012 United were in the midst of a full-scale injury crisis. The midfield had looked like the Achilles Heel for the club all season. United had had a great, gaping hole in the middle of the park when Manchester City had trounced them 6-1, in their own back yard earlier in the season. City's brick outhouse Yaya Toure and his skilful sidekick David Silva, had simply outclassed United then, and when the draw for the 3rd Round of the FA Cup was made, and it paired United with City, this time at the Etihad, many Reds had serious misgivings. We feared another thrashing was on the cards.

But, on the morning of the game, Sir Alex Ferguson sprung one of the biggest surprises in his entire reign when he produced a team-sheet which featured the name Paul Scholes. And the lift Scholes' reemergence gave to the squad allowed United to go on to beat City 3-2 (even though Scholes was immediately at fault for a City goal after he came on as a substitute).

Scholes, apparently, couldn't bear not playing, not being at the heart of things. This man, this ginger prince, who'd spent a whole career shunning the limelight, had missed the bizz of playing in front of 76,000 spectators. And so Fergie had re-registered him as a player. Given him a new contract until the end of the season. And at the end of the season, Scholes wasn't ready to quit then, either. He signed a year extension on his contract and started the 2012-13 in sparkling form as United tried desperately to wrest back the Premier League title from City. An injury in the second half of the season restricted his appearances, but he still made enough to qualify for his medal.

Scholes is loved by the fans. He's still amongst the top-selling shirts at T-Shirts United, and his song is amongst those most regularly sung at Old Trafford, even when he isn't playing: "He scores goals, my lord, he scores goals. Paul Scholes, he scores goals."

Verdict: For the second central midfielder's berth, it's yet another case of 'Sophie's Choice'. Bryan Robson and Paul Scholes both have their own

193

persuasive arguments. Both were wonderful players, both were inspirational leaders (although Scholesy was more of an inspirer through pure talent, while Robbo pulled United up by the bootstraps). Both scored important goals. Both missed matches - Robbo through injury, Scholes due to suspension.

When asked to name the best central midfielder under Sir Alex Ferguson, Norman Whiteside was definitive in his answer. "Bryan Robson, without a doubt," the Northern Irishman said. "Robbo was, no question, the best midfield player of his generation." Big Norm, of course, wasn't so bad himself, and one would do well not to get on the wrong side of the Whiteside by choosing any other candidate for the role.

And Ethel Sleith, the Branch Secretary of the Manchester United Supporters' Club, South Africa, couldn't help but agree. "Robbo and Roy," she gushed. "I'd like to see anyone get past either of them, and if they were in the same side. Wow! Both were players who could win a game single handed - and did." They were also, importantly, "players for whom the *team* came first."

But then again, on sheer appearance numbers alone, Paul Scholes should make the cut too. Scholes, like Robbo, was a player of innate talent, and natural ability, but I think Scholes was – at his height – a more creative influence than Robson. And finally, Scholes has the ultimate trump card. As an honorary member of the 'Class of '92', as a player who climbed through the ranks at United and reached the highest rung, has to take the nod. Because United's tradition of promoting and playing young players is one of the crucial things that sets us apart from the common or garden club. It is the thing that makes United the mythical team that it is today, because it harks back to our history: the Busby Babes.

United might have paid British record transfer fees for some players, like Robson, Ferdinand, Keane, and Berbatov, and Fergie might have raided the bargain bin for others, like Schmeichel, Van Der Sar, Irwin, and Solksjaer. But the players who continue the Manchester United narrative, those who continue to tell the tale of our difference from the run of the mill, are those who are, for the most part, born and bred Red, like Scholes.

Neil Custis again backs up the – somewhat controversial 'Team Fergie' argument: "In central midfield many would not look past Bryan Robson. But I would not have him in there ahead of Paul Scholes. Scholes has been described by Paddy Crerand as United's greatest ever player. A master at opening teams up and arriving late to chip in with goals himself."

Paul Scholes, he scores goals…

And it's not just Paddy Crerand believes Scholes is the "greatest". In a recent interview, United fans' hate figure Carlos Tevez was quoted as saying Paul Scholes was the best player he'd ever played alongside. Which is some statement. Especially when you consider Tevez has hardly spoken of his United years in glowing terms – he's picked fights with Gary Neville and even Sir Alex himself since departing Old Trafford for the Etihad. Especially when you consider which other *greats* Tevez has lined up alongside in his career. For Tevez has played in the same team as the two current undisputed 'best players in the world' in Leo Messi and Cristiano Ronaldo. And yet Scholes was still, for Tevez, the head and shoulders number one.

As that oft-spotted flag in the United ends of stadiums up and down the country reads: "Not Arrogant: Just Better."

FERGIE'S FINEST

9 - Left Wing

Flying wingers are a crucial component of any Manchester United side and 'Team Fergie' is no different. We've been lucky enough to have watched some brilliant wingers during the Ferguson era at Old Trafford.

There's been the Portuguese, Luis Nani, who, for performances against Arsenal alone, deserves a mention (although generally, his form has been too inconsistent – he's infuriating and effective match by match). There's been the Elvis-impersonating, Sharpey-shufflin' Lee Sharpe, whose wing wizardry in the early 1990s was a joy to watch – particularly his hat-trick when United were wearing *those* blue and white Christmas-tree style shirts as United thrashed Arsenal 6-2 in the League Cup at Highbury in the 1990-91 season.

But one player stands head and shoulders above the rest. And not just above the rest of the United wingers, but every other player who has ever played in the Premier League. And so, with this in mind, and to recognise that player's achievements in

198

a Red shirt, this is the only position in 'Team Fergie' which is not open to any debate. Debate would be stupid. Pointless.

As Phil Martin says: "Despite constant grumblings amongst a minority of reds, Giggs has undoubtedly been the best left winger for at least two decades; you'll miss him when he's gone!" Ethel Sleith, Branch Secretary of the Manchester United Supporters' Club, South Africa agrees: "Ryan plays with the interest of the team at heart," and is "United through and through." Tina Turner would describe Giggsy as "Simply the Best".

Ryan Giggs

Picture the scene. It is March 2nd 1991. *The Grifters* and *Green Card* are showing at the brand-spanking new multiplex cinema. Families have their Saturday tea in front of *Noel's House Party* on the telly. 'Do the Bartman' by The Simpsons is at number one in the charts. Everyone's obsessed by playing Sonic the Hedgehog on the Sega Megadrive. And if that

199

enough Peter Kay-a-like nostalgia for you, how about this sobering thought: at the time, Manchester United had seven top division championships to their name, and one European Cup. The last time their name had been carved into the trophy of each competition, however, was back in the 1960's.

The past, as the novelist L. P. Hartley contended, really was a "foreign country". They really did "do things differently there." I mean, did we ever really watch *Noel's House Party?* Did we really buy enough copies of 'Do the Bartman' to make it top of the hit parade? Were United ever really that down in the dumps?

Well, the short answer is yes. But on March 2nd 1991 everything changed when a handsome young chap with hair like spirali pasta took the field at Old Trafford as a late substitute for the injured Denis Irwin in a 2-0 defeat for United against Everton. The replacement's name was Ryan Giggs. We were to hear it quite a lot over the next twenty-two years. And although he couldn't affect the end result of *that* match, soon he was leaving his own, indelible stamp on the English game. For Giggsy has not so much raised the bar in terms of his achievements — there is a whole page on Wikipedia dedicated to the records he's set as a player – but blasted that bar off into space. No player will ever surpass what Giggs has done as a player.

Nobody.

Arsenal FC are one of the grandest names in world football. They are the third-most decorated club in the English game. They were founded in 1886, and in their proud 127-year history they have won 13 league championships. Ryan Giggs has won exactly the same, in 22 years.

He's also stuffed away two Champions League winner's medals, four FA Cup winner's medals, three League Cup winner's medals, two (consecutive) PFA Young Player of the Year awards, one PFA Player of the Year award, an OBE, and the BBC Sports Personality of the Year award.

Ryan Giggs is cultural and football phenomenon. One teacher in the Leamington Spa area a few years back was amused to discover that she had three Ryans in her new class. Not only that, she also had a kid named Ryangiggs: all one word. Like a brand, a guarantee of greatness. They talk about him in Parliament. He has made the most Premier League appearances of any player, and, when he scored against Everton in February 2013, he became the only player to have scored in every Premier League season (his full record is a goal in 23 consecutive seasons in the top division). He has started more times than any other player for Manchester United FC.

He was an obvious choice to be inducted into the National Football Museum's Hall of Fame. The criteria for entry is thus: players have to be over 30 and have to have played more than 5 years in English football. Giggs was chosen by a Selection Panel led by Sir Bobby Charlton – whose United appearance record he shattered – and his selection can only be described as a 'no-brainer'. (Incidentally, the other Ferguson-era United players selected for the Hall of Fame thus far include: Peter Schmeichel, Bryan Robson, Roy Keane, Paul Scholes, Ryan Giggs, David Beckham, Teddy Sheringham, Eric Cantona, and Mark Hughes. This would make a pretty handy 'Team Fergie' actually, although for the moment it looks a little light on defenders.)

Giggs credits yoga for helping with his incredible longevity. It has helped him to manage his body in order to keep up with the extreme demands of the modern game. He's also constantly, and successfully, reinvented himself. From young tyro to elder statesman. From the frizzy-haired, smouldering young poster boy for a generation of teenage girls across Manchester and beyond to the silver fox, who, when he takes a corner in front of you, shows an obvious bald patch. From the flying winger to the wily midfield schemer. Sir Alex Ferguson, jubilant after United's thirteenth league triumph on April 22nd 2013, called Giggs his "freak". But in a good way, obviously. The National Football Museum could have inducted three Giggsys such has been his impact on the game. He's set records at both ends of the scale, as both the youngest, and the oldest.

But we'll start with the young tyro, who burst onto the scene in 1991 with the pace of Sonic the Hedgehog (Giggs was the son of the Cardiff RFC rugby union player, Danny Wilson, and was blessed with his father's lightning-quick speed and trademark body swerve), the impudence of Bart Simpson, and the ability of George Best (to whom Giggsy was often initially compared). Giggsy had signed for United on his 14th birthday; Fergie putting in a personal appearance at young Ryan's house to ensure he chose United over City, for whom he'd turned out in a number of schoolboy matches. And there's surely a case to be made for the fact that

City's losing out on Giggs was *the* biggest mistake of the twentieth century, even bigger than Decca missing out on the Beatles. All of which makes Ryan's subsequent success for the Reds even more delicious for United fans, who sang with extra relish (to the tune of Robin Hood): "Ryan Giggs, Ryan Giggs, running down the wing. (x2). Feared by the blues, loved by the Reds. Ryan Giggs, Ryan Giggs, Ryan Giggs."

Giggs was 17 when he made his United debut against Everton. Two months later, he was giving City their first taste of what they were missing when he scored his first goal for United *against* City at Old Trafford. It was the winner in a 1-0 victory. And, though Giggs wasn't selected in the squad for the European Cup Winners' Cup final in Rotterdam – Lee Sharpe was picked ahead of him – by the following season, Giggs was seriously cementing his place in the first team line-up. And in the season after that, Ryan helped United win their eighth league championship: their first since the sixties.

This period, in addition to being defined by Giggs winning trophies, was also defined by Alex Ferguson's protection of the player. Fergie wouldn't allow journalists any access to the young star until he turned 20, preferring him to concentrate on his game, and, behind the scenes, Sir Alex set about ensuring Giggs wouldn't fall into bad ways. There were close shaves and embarrassments, of course. Lee Sharpe often refers to the time when a purple-faced Fergie gate-crashed a party at his pad and gave him the full hair-dryer treatment. Giggsy was at the same party: hiding upstairs in a wardrobe. But when you compare Giggs' career with those of other young stars who've often fallen to temptation – *like* Sharpe, who often ended up like the kid holding the stone when the adults came along to ask questions about the broken-window - you realise just how influential Sir Alex has been. Sure he kept Giggs strangely cosseted as though he were some crazed and over-protective father, forcing Ryan to hide out in wardrobes, but now Ryan's full-to-bursting trophy cabinet, his football CV, and his sheer, extended brilliance, are surely testament to the fact Fergie did the right thing by Giggs. (And interestingly now Giggsy is playing the role of elder statesman, advising the new United starlets on how to conduct themselves. This role will become even more important now Fergie has retired.)

The coming of the second Ryan Giggs came in 1999, when United were *en route* to the treble.

Ryan was no longer the 'boyband' idol of the side: that role was now squarely occupied by one David Beckham. United faced Arsenal in the semi-final of the FA Cup at Villa Park. The first game ended in a draw, meaning that the tie would be replayed: making it the last ever FA Cup semi-final replay before the FA abolished them. With Europe in mind, Fergie juggled the squad and selected a slightly weakened team, leaving out Cole and Yorke and opting for Solksjaer and Sheringham in their stead. But there was nothing weak about the performance. Indeed, many fellow United fans have dubbed the game one of the most outstanding they have ever witnessed. And it took a moment of Giggs genius to settle it.

Arsenal were a wonderful side then. They had all the skills of the current side, but a mental and physical toughness too. And there was a sense that the semi-final would decide more than just who progressed through to the FA Cup final: it would also decide who would go on and win the Premier League title too. The momentum gained by winning such a 'clash of the Titans', and the slump which would be inspired by a loss, meant that victory was crucial. The pressure got to some players. Keane was sent-off. Phil Neville conceded a late penalty which would be taken by Denis Bergkamp. If the Dutchman scored, Arsenal would surely secure a 2-1 win. But Peter Schmeichel saved the penalty and United's ten men staggered on into extra-time.

Even then, there was no sense of what was to come. United players were dead on their feet. Some were suffering from cramp. The only hope, it seemed, was to keep Arsenal out and limp on to the lottery of a penalty shoot-out. Ryan Giggs had different ideas. Patrick Vieira tried a 'Hollywood' pass on the halfway line ("Vieira, wo-oh-oh, Vieira, wo-oh-oh. He gave Giggsy the ball, and Arsenal won f**k all."). Giggsy intercepted, picking it up in mid-stride. He was already accelerating. His pace took him past first one defender, then another. (And remember, this was *the famous* Arsenal defence: the meanest in the land: the one containing Adams, Dixon, Keown, Winterburn). And then he was weaving into the penalty area. He seemed to have taken it too wide though, and there were some in the United end behind that goal who yelled at Ryan to take the ball into the corner, to waste a little more time in order that we could make it to penalties.

But Giggs didn't listen. He hit a rocket of a left-footer past the England goalkeeper David

Seaman and into the roof of the net and sent United fans into ecstasy. Giggs himself seemed completely overwhelmed by the magnitude, the wonder, of his strike. The lad was usually a cool customer when it came to goal celebrations. There'd be a lugubrious arm in the air, or else a rehearsed dance with Paul Ince. But here Giggsy's head 'went'. He set off on another mad run, removing his white shirt as he went. And then twirling it over his head like some demented cheerleader. But what was most striking was the hairy chest he revealed. I mean, it was like a rainforest. There were whole, undiscovered ecosystems on his torso. This was Giggsy the man, not the boy wonder.

But Giggsy the man was now being judged as a man. Fans are more forgiving of kids, especially those who've come through the ranks. But now, spoiled by years of consistent form from the number 11, United fans began to mutter their discontent at every misplaced pass, every miscued cross. After the treble, Giggsy entered the wilderness years. To some, he had a new name. He was now known as 'Bloody hell Giggs'. The Welshman celebrated a decade at United with a testimonial against Celtic, however, his 2001-02 campaign was to be his poorest at United as he struggled to recapture his form. He'd perhaps lost a yard of pace. He couldn't just knock the ball past the full-back and blaze past them any more. For the first time, there was a need for him to reinvent his game in order to maintain his high standards.

And over the next few seasons, we saw Giggs moving further and further inside until, in 2008-09, he began playing 'in the hole' behind the strikers. And he began to make that role his own too. The football knowledge he'd picked up throughout his long career meant he saw gaps others might not have done, and his passing improved immeasurably. 2008 brought his second Champions League medal and *another* League title and then, in 2009, he began to receive award after award mostly in recognition of his 'lifetime achievement'. Lifetime achievement awards are generally given to those approaching the twilight years of their careers, and indeed, from 2009, Giggs was only ever offered one-year contract extensions by the club. But as each season rolls on to the next, he's shown no signs he will "go gentle into that good night" of retirement.

Instead he rages "against the dying of the light", a "freak", a vintage wine, a man for all seasons.

Giggsy signed his most recent contract with United in March 2013. It will keep him at the club until the end of the 2013-14 season, by which time he'll be 40. And the next record he'll have in his sight is surely Edwin Van Der Sar's record of being the second oldest player to compete in a Champions League final. Or maybe he's looking further into the distance. Maybe he's aiming for another five years at United. Maybe he's hoping he'll equal *Liverpool's* record of 18 league championships all on his own.

If Ryan Giggs was a club, he'd be as successful as Arsenal, and rapidly catching Liverpool up. If he was a club, he would be hugely well supported. Giggsy's popularity is enduring: Hugh Evans of SoccerStarz, which make footballer figurines, says that they "have only been around since August last year and so far the top selling player United player is Wayne Rooney, followed by Kagawa (SoccerStarz are massive in Japan), Giggs, and Ferguson himself." If Ryan Giggs was a club, he'd have won more top flight matches than about a quarter of the Premier League sides he faced in the 2012-13 season.

You don't get many calling him "Bloody Hell Giggs" any more.

Verdict: Ryan Giggs. 'Nuff said. As the banner in the Sir Alex Ferguson Stand says: "Giggs: Tearing you apart since 1991."

10 - Striker

Football formations fall in and out of fashion. It used to be the received wisdom that a team played a simple 4-4-2 with two up top. One of those two was a big guy, a brick outhouse who'd win headers against the opposition centre-half, knocking them down for his smaller, terrier-like partner. Now there's a trend for playing one up front, on his own, or even, in the case of Barcelona, no nominal striker at all.

So is the striker dead? Not at Old Trafford he's not. 4-4-2 remains the classic default for a Ferguson United team, and Sir Alex is the most successful manager ever in the English game. And though he tinkered with a 4-4-1-1, or a 4-5-1, especially in Europe, at the Theatre of Dreams, more often than not, we came to see United as they'd always been. The flying wingers. The creative-destructive central midfield axis. The two forwards. Of course, Ferguson's never been one for the Big-Guy, Little-Guy combo. At United, you'll most often see a highly-skilled, deep-lying forward playing just behind a more predatory "fox in the box". Here, we'll take a look at the contenders for the role of the 'number 10' in 'Fergie's Finest' x11.

Mark Hughes

Roberto Carlos aside, Mark Hughes surely had the biggest thighs in the history of football. I mean they were *huge*. The size of giant redwood treetrunks. Bulging with muscles. Bristling with intent. They were the pistons which helped him to power-in some of the greatest goals ever seen from a Manchester United forward. They must have struck terror into even the hardiest of opposition defenders. Even though – facially – Sparky resembled Ailsa from *Home and Away,* when they took in the rest of this fearsome physical specimen, goalkeepers must have wanted to pull on bigger, more padded gloves just to protect their fingers from being broken.

Hughesie's love affair with Manchester United has been a tempestuous one. The Welshman

213

twice left the club as a player – and most United legends don't get the opportunity to go back – and also stained his reputation by playing for Chelsea, and later, by managing Manchester City, but the memories of his great goals – and Hughes was famously a scorer of great goals rather than a great goalscorer – still keeps many a United fan warm at night.

He was famous for his acrobatic volleys, for his fierce half-volleys, for his overhead kicks, his scissor-kicks. He scored wonder goals at Wembley, in finals and semi-finals. He scored the 'consolation' goal in an horrific 5-1 defeat against Manchester City (though United fans can laugh at the fact that Hughes' goal is generally the only one remembered from that game, above all five of theirs.) And he scored a brace on that famous night in Rotterdam, when United secured the first European trophy of the Sir Alex Ferguson years.

Hughes began life at Manchester United after leaving school in 1980. The Wrexham-born star's first-team debut came three years later, in a League Cup tie against Oxford United. Quickly, he forged a decent partnership with United's former Arsenal striker Frank Stapleton. And in 1984-85,

Sparky began to sparkle in the United front-line, smashing in an impressive 25 goals in all competitions as Ron Atkinson's Reds finished fourth in the league and reached the FA Cup final (they beat Everton 1-0, through a goal by Norman Whiteside, who'd been shunted back out of attack and into midfield to accommodate Hughes' emergence).

Off the back of the 1985 FA Cup win, United started the 1985-86 season like a train, with Sparky's goals helping United to an unbelievable start of ten straight wins in the league. This was a feat which allowed some fans to dare to dream of a first league title since 1967. United continued to lead the pack until February, but the Reds' form fell away and United ended up finishing a disappointing fourth. The reasons for this precipitate decline were legion, but one can point the finger at internal strife as one of the chief contributing factors. You see, in around February – coincidence? - rumours had begun to surface, linking United's Welsh tyro with a move to Barcelona – who could promise European football: English clubs were banned from European competition after the Heysel disaster of 1985 – and United, and Hughes, were distracted. Took their eye off the First Division ball. And, come the end of the season, the rumour mill was, for once, proved correct: Hughesie moved to Barca for £2 million. It was suggested the deal had been done some time in January-February, but had been kept private.

In 1985-86, Hughes had bagged an impressive 17 league goals for Big Ron's Reds. It would be his best ever season in terms of goal-scoring. At Barcelona, however, he was a failure. Signed to partner Gary Lineker, he simply couldn't find his form, or goal-scoring touch, and Terry Venables, the then Barca manager, eventually sent Hughes out on loan to Bayern Munich.

And then, the return of the Prodigal Son. Re-signing Hughes must have been a 'no-brainer' for Alex Ferguson – who'd replaced Ron Atkinson in 1986 – and in May 1988, he splashed out a club record £1.8 million to bring back the much-loved star. And in 1988-89, it seemed money well-spent: Hughes went on to be voted PFA Player of the Year (the first United player in history to win it) and then, in 1989-90, even more shrewd, when Hughes helped United secure the first piece of silverware under Sir Alex, when they won the FA Cup against Crystal Palace. Hughes scored twice in the final, which

216

finished 3-3, before a Lee Martin goal won the replay.

Then, in 1990-91, came Rotterdam. And, as fate would have it, United face Barcelona in the final of the European Cup Winners' Cup, at the Feijenoord Stadium on 15th May. Desperate to prove he was a more talented player than the Catalans had seen during his disappointing spell at Camp Nou, he played like a lion in the final. He showed all the accomplishments United fans had become accustomed to seeing: he held the ball up majestically, proved impossible to knock off it. He harried and pressed the Barcelona defenders. He brought his teammates into play. But he also showed a heretofore unseen poacher's instinct. In the 67th minute, Steve Bruce headed a Bryan Robson free-kick goalwards. It was going in anyway. It was virtually over the line. And yet Hughesie threw himself at the ball and provided the final touch, to ensure his name got on the score-sheet (and settled a few scores to boot).

Better was to come from Hughes six minutes later when, clear through on the Barcelona goal, he prodded the ball past the Catalan 'keeper, but seemed to have taken it too wide. But Hughes adjusted his position and, with the outside of his boot, curled the ball back into the goal from an almost impossibly tight angle. It was a wonderful goal, and would later prove to be the winner, after Koeman pulled one back for Barcelona.

United had won their first European trophy under Fergie, and this against a Barcelona team boasting the myriad talents of Michael Laudrup, Ronald Koeman, and, in goal, Carles Busquets (whose son Sergio played in the two Barcelona-Manchester United Champions League finals in 2009 and 2011).

And Hughes finished the season on a high on a personal note when he was again voted PFA Player of the Year.

The following season saw United heart-breakingly lose out to Leeds United in the league championship race, but in 1992-93, Hughes was to win his first Premier League winner's medal with the Reds. And in 1993-94, United won the first double in the club's history. Hughesie scored in both the FA Cup final – in which United strolled to a 4-0 win against Chelsea – and the League Cup final – in which a ten-man United lost 3-1 against Aston Villa. He'd also scored a cracking, season-defining last-minute volleyed equalizer against Oldham Athletic in the FA Cup final that year. Just like with the Arsenal semi-final in 1999, you got the impression that had they *lost* that game, the Reds might well have ended the season empty handed. But Hughes' treetrunk thighs had seen to that. Outside Wembley, I bumped into Red legend Paddy Crerand. He put his hand on his chest. Said: "*Close, bloody hell!?!*" A figure of speech which would find an echo in Fergie's comments after the 1999 Champions League final: "Football, eh? Bloody hell."

United so often have the will to find a way in these matches which go down to the wire. And it's not luck. It is drive. Desire. Hunger. The players not wanting to trudge back into that dressing room to face Fergie, empty-handed.

But that's exactly what happened the following season. United so nearly won the double-double, but a draw against West Ham when only a win would do in the league, and a 1-0 defeat against Everton in the FA Cup final saw the Reds lose out. And at the end of the season, Fergie tore up the blueprint and started again, giving youth - in the form of Paul Scholes, David Beckham, Gary Neville, and Phil Neville – a chance. Hughes, along with

Kanchelskis and Ince, was to leave the club in the summer of 1994: Sparky went to Chelsea for a fee of £1.5 million.

Fittingly for a man who played, and scored, in a lot of cup finals, Hughesie's last game in a Red shirt had come at Wembley.

Dwight Yorke

Some players have the pleasure of playing top-level football for one of the biggest clubs in the world. They get paid handsomely for it. They carry off trophies. They are adored by thousands, if not millions. And yet they look as though they have been press-ganged into it. They look as though they detest every minute. You watch their faces. They sigh and sneer their way through the pre-match warm up. Snarl and moan their way through the game itself. Spit and groan through their post-match interviews.

Dwight Yorke was not one of those players. Dwight Yorke played with a full-beam smile on his face, hardly caring that his wonky teeth were on show. He looked as though he was having the time of his life, as though United was a totally tropical beach (or perhaps a beautiful woman). He'd pull off a trick, make a fool of some poor sap of an unsmiling defender, and the camera would catch that mischievous gleam in Yorkie's eyes. He looked as though he wanted to roar with laughter.

But if you made the mistake of underestimating Dwight, of reading him as some kind of show-boating fool, then you were on a sticky wicket. For Brian Lara's best mate was sparklingly skilful, devastatingly destructive, and an instinctive finisher of the highest order. Sure he was full of flicks and tricks. But he was also all about doing the simple things very, very well. If he was presented with a goal-scoring opportunity, you could rest assured he wouldn't simply bat it out of the ground. Rather, he'd place it, with unerring accuracy. And have a good time dispatching it too. And the greatest thing about Yorke was the bigger the stage, the better time he had. And when Yorkie was having fun, you could pretty much guarantee United fans were too.

Dwight Eversley Yorke – his name sounds like some unholy supergroup consisting of Reg

221

Dwight, the Everley brothers, and maybe Dwight Yoakam: and perhaps that's what Yorkie's been laughing at all these years – was born on Tobago. Graham 'Do I Not Like That' Taylor 'discovered' him when his Aston Villa side were on tour of the West Indies in 1989. Yorke was quickly offered a trial, in which he impressed, and he was soon part of the Villa squad, where he spent a successful nine years before his move to Old Trafford. Indeed, until very recently, Yorkie was Villa's all-time leading scorer in the Premier League, with 60 goals, until Agbonlahor overtook his tally on 29th April 2013.

His form at Villa Park convinced Fergie that the time was right for the Tobagan to make the step up, and join Manchester United. But the then Villa manager, John Gregory played hard-ball. He wanted Andy Cole in exchange for Yorke. Deal or no deal? United were, understandably, deterred by Gregory's stance. But Yorke was, by this time, desperate to join the Old Trafford side, and he was rumoured to have knocked on Gregory's office door and demanded a move. Gregory later said that had he had a gun in his office, he would quite happily have shot Dwight.

Eventually though, in August 1998, an unscathed, perhaps bullet-proof Yorke joined United for £12.6 million. And United fans immediately had a new hero. They couldn't resist reminding Gregory of the transfer saga either. He was instantly granted a terrace chant, to the tune of *Lord of the Dance:* "Dwight Yorke, wherever you may be, you are the King of pornography, and you stuck two fingers up at John Gregory, Now you play for the MUFC."

He was to pay United fans back for our initial enthusiasm for him in manifold ways, as he smiled his way to a devastating first season with the Reds, in which United swept all before them on course to an unprecedented treble. He was our Premier League top-scorer that fateful season, weighing in with an impressive 18 goals. But it was his imperious form in the Champions League – in which he scored in the back yards of the biggest clubs on the European stage in Bayern Munich, Barcelona, Internazionale and Juventus – which cemented Yorkie's place as a bonafide United hero. And, even more impressive than that was the *way* he took the game to these European giants. In an almost telepathic partnership with his new pal, Andy Cole, the deadly duo tore into defences across the continent. They showcased a brilliant array of combination plays, from *tika-taka* one-twos to reverse passes to flicks. They tore defences apart.

223

They seemed to have as much fun creating for each other as they did in scoring themselves.

The Barcelona game in particular was telling. Though it was 'only' a group stage match, it was to prove crucial in United's throwing-off of the inferiority complex which had dogged them throughout their European campaigns of the 1990s. Then the 'foreigners' ruling had always dictated the team Fergie could pick. And hamstrung the Reds. Sir Alex usually had to leave out at least one star: be it Hughes, Cantona, Kanchelskis, Keane. Or Schmeichel, who Fergie had to leave out back in 1994, when a domestically dominant United with squad 'keeper Gary Walsh in goal went on to be humiliated 4-0 at Camp Nou. So in 1999 when United returned, they were still feeling their way into European competition. And there was a strong sense the team felt intimidated. Reluctant to show-off the skills they'd honed in the Premier League. They crept into their shells and played in a wholly unfamiliar 'safety-first' way, which, as we all know is most definitely not the United way. But that night, Yorke and Cole played some of the best attacking football ever seen by men in Red, on the biggest of stages. They played like kids on a beach, having fun. And though a late Barcelona equalizer robbed them of a victory, it was the game that finally convinced the young squad that they really could compete with the best.

And *beat* them too.

There was no hangover in Yorkie's second season either, as United *blitzed* the Premier League, with Dwight netting 22 goals in all competitions. The only dampener was in the Champions League, when a Fernando Redondo-inspired Real Madrid knocked the Reds out at the quarter-final stage. But although it was not immediately apparent to fans, Fergie noticed a 'slackening' in the Tobagan's desire during his third season at Old Trafford. Yorkie's extra-curricular activities – this isn't *Hello,* I won't mention one particular glamour model's name here – were apparently starting to take their toll. That drive, which Fergie expected from all of his players, was dwindling.

And of course, Sir Alex never waited for the moment that fire burns out. He acted quickly. Yorke was sold to Blackburn in 2002, for £2 million. He just missed out on a hundred league games for United, and had an excellent goals per game ratio which, until Ronaldo and Messi decided to redefine the rules, was a brilliant one-in-two. He won three

Premier League titles, one Champions League, and one FA Cup during his time at Old Trafford.

And no, he never did stop smiling.

Wayne Rooney

Wayne Rooney hardly *looks* like a comic-book hero. Unless you're thinking of Shrek. You can hardly imagine him modelling pants, like Becks, and if you can, then you might want to wash your brain out with Listerine afterwards. Unlike Giggsy, he didn't have a springy mop of spirali pasta frizzing behind him when he made a run. No, Roo was receding badly. Had been, it looked like, since he was about ten. And if Ole Gunnar Solksjaer was the baby-faced assassin, Wayne Rooney joined United as the "assassin-faced baby". All lantern-jawed, like Desperate Dan. All mean-eyed. All barrel-chested. Steven Wells of *The Guardian,* memorably described the Roonbat as "a tightly muscled slab of crocodilian cunning, carnivorous aggression and ruthless malevolence."

Having joined United in 2004, the dead-eyed Rooney has ruthlessly set about winning 5 Premier League titles, one Champions League title, two League Cups, and a FIFA Club World Cup. He's also won numerous individual honours and has scored many, many decisive goals (in total, he's three short of two hundred for the Reds).

To opposition fans at least, then, Rooney is in fact the ultimate villain. Especially to our "noisy neighbours" Manchester City, against whom Rooney, at 27, has already bagged an impressive 10 goals. This is Leigh Fairhurst on the United number 10: "As a Manchester City fan there have been many United players who have had the ability to silence me - or cause me to grimace as though someone was holding a shotgun to my face with the trigger half-pulled - when they receive the ball in or around the penalty area. Hughes, Cantona, Scholes, Beckham, Van Nistelrooy, Giggsy, Ronaldo to name but a few. But one player in particular always has, and unfortunately for me, *still will* have the ability (for another 10 or 12 years yet, if Giggsy's playing

227

record is anything to go by) to bring a grown man to his knees."

And he goes by the name of Wayne Rooney.

"Since he opened his Manchester derby goal-scoring account back in February 2005, at the ripe age of 19, I just knew this lad was going to ruin a few derby days for me. Not that United had *needed* a Rooney prior to this to spoil the day anyway, but his arrival meant at least a decade of unnecessary wear and tear on the old ticker."

"Rooney is the player I dread around the edge of our box. He's the one who can pull that trigger in a split second and shoot down my hopes. His goals make me suffer that familiar long-stare at the ground in the middle of the pub, whilst the majority of my United mates celebrate around me. Rooney constantly reminds me I might have made something of a bad choice when I was 8 years old and I was deciding which club to follow."

Perhaps Rooney's most fondly remembered derby strike came in February 2011, at Old Trafford. Going into the match the Roonster had a poor record – 5 goals all season – however Leigh still "just knew he would ruin my day..." And he did, "with a strike that no other man on the planet would have had the stupidity to even attempt in fear of the embarrassment when the ball hits row Z. A scissors-kick volley that no football fan will ever forget." It was a truly awesome goal in an otherwise forgettable performance from United's number 10. Ignore all those gibes about it being "a shinner". This was the goal of the season and *one of* the goals of the century.

That City goal could have come straight from Pele's repertoire. And the Pele comparison was one that certainly did the rounds when Roo-Mania first hit the Premier League. And though Rooney might not have hit the exalted heights some predicted in his early flush of form, the United fans still sing about 'the white Pele'. ("Saw my Mate, the other day; Said to me he'd seen the white Pele. So I asked 'Who is he?', He goes by the name of Wayne Rooney. Wayne Rooney, Wayne Rooney, He goes by the name of Wayne Rooney."

Another side which had good reason to shrink at the very sight of United's ogre-ish centre forward was Newcastle United, against whom Rooney had a startling record. Roo didn't just score a great number of goals against Newcastle, he was also a scorer of *great goals* against them. Andy Rivers, author of the Newcastle United-inspired *I'm Rivelinho,* observes: "Rooney went through a period where he would volley the ball from about two miles out into the top corner of our net every time we played Manchester United. We've had some decent keepers at Newcastle over the last decade but none of them got near any of these efforts. I'm glad he gets played on the wing a lot now."

Wazza has haunted the nightmares of many other sides since he first exploded onto the scene in 2002 with Everton. Then, at the tender age of 16, the boy from Croxteth had the body of the 27-year-old he is now, and he had absolutely no fear. He made his senior debut, becoming the second youngest first-team player in Everton history, on 17th August, at home to Spurs in a match which ended 2–2. And then, on 2nd October, scored his first senior goals with a brace in a League Cup tie against Wrexham. But then came the *coup de theatre.* Two weeks later, Arsenal visited Goodison Park on the crest of a wave – they hadn't been beaten in 30 games. And Rooney, still a week before his 17th birthday, scored a stunning last-gasp winner. Rooney also made his first appearance at Old Trafford that season (although wearing the wrong colours: "Once a blue, always a Red").

In a brief cameo, one of the very first things he did was embark on one of his trademark runs - think the ones he made for England in the European Championships, or for United v Newcastle, or Arsenal practically every time the Reds played them. And though he couldn't round off this fine run with a goal, he'd certainly set Sir Alex's antennae twitching. The next thing Rooney did was to launch into a clumsy-looking 'tackle', one straight from the Paul Scholes handbook, which might have brought him a red card.

But then, Rooney has always walked the tightrope between brilliance and madness. In August 2004, United beat off Newcastle to the signature of the much-vaunted young star. Wazza signed for a mammoth fee of £25.6 million – then a record for a teenager – and his debut at Old Trafford – wearing the number 8 shirt - came under the floodlights in the Champions League, with a group stage match against Fenerbahce on 28th September. Rooney was absolutely magnificent that night: unplayable. He scored a hat-trick - some tally for European debut in anyone's book, let alone a teenager's (and with the trio, he became the youngest player to score a hat-trick in Champions League history) - but his performance was about so much more than just the goals. Indeed Rooney got so caught up in the moment that at one point, it seemed to slip his mind which way United were kicking, and he attempted an audacious shot - against his own goalkeeper - from the halfway line which thankfully went out for a corner. Again, the brilliance and the madness.

Ultimately though, the Roonster's first season at Old Trafford was not a successful one for the club. United finished third in the Premier League, and were knocked out at the quarter-final stage of the Champions League. They lost in the League Cup semi-final against Chelsea, and the FA Cup final against Arsenal, in Cardiff, on penalties. Rooney himself had had a promising first year though: he was the Red Devils' top-scorer in the Premier League, hitting double figures for the first time as a senior player, and he walked away with the PFA Young Player of the Year Award.

And things would get better. Rooney won his first trophy as United blitzed Wigan Athletic in the final of the 2006 League Cup. And though the Abramovich bank-rolled and Mourinho-coached Chelsea won the league that year, in the next season, a Rooney and Ronaldo-inspired United won "our trophy back", and Wazza had his first (of five)

Premier League winner's medals. Then, in 2007-08, United went one better, by beating Chelsea to both the league title and the Champions League.

But, though Rooney continued to improve, season-on-season, in terms of his goals scored for the side, during this period Rooney slipped *behind* Ronaldo in terms of importance to the team. Though the pair were once thought to have similarly bright futures, it was now clear that Sir Alex Ferguson intended to build his team around the Portuguese star, rather than the lad from Croxteth. Sir Alex allowed Ronaldo a free, roaming role in the side which meant that more discipline was required of Rooney. Indeed, Wazza often found himself playing out of position on the wing, as he did in the Champions League final against Barcelona in Rome in 2009.

But when Ronaldo left, shortly after that Rome final, Wayne Rooney found himself suddenly United's *main man* again. And how he revelled in it. He practically won the league single-handed that year. Or at least in cahoots with Antonio Valencia, who'd come in from Wigan to replace Ronaldo on the right-wing. Midway through the season, Rooney had a remarkable run of goals. Sir Alex Ferguson

233

observed that Rooney scores in spurts, in gluts, but even by Wazza's standards, this was something else. And what was most remarkable was that nearly every one of these goals was scored with his head. We all knew Rooney was *good* with his head, but suddenly he was world class. There was a spell in 2010 when Rooney scored with his head every week, usually from a pinpoint Valencia cross. And it wasn't just on the domestic front. No, Rooney translated his form for the European stage, scoring two headers in United's 3-2 win at the San Siro against AC Milan. Two weeks later, it was his header that won the Reds the League Cup at Wembley, against Aston Villa. United won the Premier League and League Cup that season, and were unlucky in the Champions League – if not for Rafael's unfortunate sending-off against Bayern Munich at Old Trafford in the quarter-final, who was to say United wouldn't have at least reached the final?

And if I'd have been asked to pick 'Team Fergie' back in 2010, Wayne Rooney would have been very much the first, or maybe second name on the team sheet. However, in October 2010, when a very watery-eyed Alex Ferguson gave a press conference in which he dropped the bombshell that Wayne Rooney wanted to leave United. There were strong rumours there was another club involved. Sickeningly, it soon became clear that the club in question were the newly petro-dollar rich "noisy neighbours", Manchester City, for whom Roon had previously been the number 1 pantomime villain. It couldn't be happening, could it?

There followed a horrible spell of claim and counter-claim. Rooney had been dropped for a previous game because of injury. Rooney hadn't been injured at all. Rooney wanted to leave for money. Rooney wanted to leave because he thought United lacked ambition – they weren't signing the right level of Class A player.

Of course, we all know now about Rooney's dramatic u-turn. Two days after Sir Alex's emotional press conference, Rooney backtracked, agreed to sign a brand new five-year contract with the Old Trafford club, thus preventing what would have been a major coup, a statement of intent, for Manchester City.

But those few October days changed everything. Though United fans still sing Rooney's name just as they always have, it's not with the same gusto it once was. Though he's still revered for his goal-scoring, there are new mutterings about his all-round contribution to the team. And every time he is substituted, or misses a match through injury, there are whisperings of a new rift with Fergie. Many won't forgive him for his dalliance with City, agent-talk though it might have been. And we certainly won't forget the sight of Sir Alex, so clearly shell-shocked, talking of how Rooney wanted to leave. It's the state of football now. We've been spoiled with one-club servants like Giggsy, Scholes, and Gary Neville. We have to expect players will leave. Ronaldo left. But still, the Rooney-City saga left a very nasty taste in the mouth.

Rooney's still popular amongst young fans, of course. I spoke with Hugh Evans of SoccerStarz, the manufacturers of 'football figurines'. The company "have only been around since August last year and so far the top selling player Man Utd player is Wayne Rooney followed by Kagawa (SoccerStarz are massive in Japan), Giggs and Ferguson himself." But amongst hardcore Reds? Bridges have been burned.

There's one fitting afterword to the Wayne Rooney story. During all of those contract negotiations back in 2010, Rooney often claimed that the club "failed to match his own ambition". He said United never went in for top-top players any more. Well, in response to Manchester City's pipping United to the title on goal difference in 2012, that was exactly what Ferguson did. He went out and paid top dollar for the top scorer in the Premier League, one Robin Van Persie. And suddenly United had another Class A player. And suddenly the new Class A player replaced the old one. It was Robin Van Persie who was suddenly the number one forward at United.

Sometimes you have to be careful what you wish for. Sometimes there really is a comic-book hero waiting around the corner.

Eric Cantona

With all due respect to a certain John Winston Lennon, to most United fans, Eric 'the King' Cantona is bigger than Jesus and the Beatles all rolled into one.

Amongst United fans, he's attained the status of a religious icon. Some still refer to him as "God". Legendary United fan and songsmith Pete Boyle was pictured in a couple of club documentaries about Cantona prostrating himself in front of an Eric billboard – the famous Nike one: "66 was a great year for English football. Eric was born". One of the many, many United songs dedicated to the man, the legend, paints Eric as Christ: "What a friend we have in Jesus, he's our Saviour from afar. What a friend we have in Jesus, and his name is Cantona." And upon the Frenchman's return to the playing squad after his lengthy ban for kicking a fan, Eric's 'comeback' was described in at least two Sky Sports interviews prior to the Liverpool game as "like the Second Coming of Christ."

Yeah, Reds tend to get a little silly where Eric the King is concerned…

The only thing in world football that comes close to comparing with United's worshipping of King Eric is the way Napoli fans still revere Maradona. Hell, they've even registered 'Maradona' as an official religion in Argentina. (Interestingly Cantona and Maradona started an unofficial Players Union between them in the 1990s. They were like a Union of Superheroes. The Union of Extraordinary Footballers.)

Make no mistake about it, Cantona was, and still is, loved. We loved him for the way he played with his chest puffed out and his collar turned up. We loved him for the goals he scored and for those he created. We loved him because he talked about "seagulls" and "trawlers" rather than a footballer's usual stock platitudes. We loved him for securing the double-double, against Liverpool, of all clubs, at Wembley, of all places, in the last minute. We loved him because he loved us: here was an artist who'd found his canvas at Old Trafford, who found his audience in us, the Red fans. We loved him because he wore the number 7 shirt like Robbo, like Georgie Best. We loved him because he *wasn't* Jesus. No, he had the Red Devil in him. He could get p***ed off, lash out. Stamp. Rage. And when he did so, he didn't simply try a sly elbow as most footballers would. No, he launched himself into the b***dy crowd, *kung-fu* kicked them into submission.

He captured the imagination. John Hegley, one of the nation's foremost innovative comic poets, memorably penned a slice of magical surrealism which talked-up Cantona as "My Grandma's favourite footballer by far". It was a poem fitting of the kind of stuff Eric himself often spouted (when you weren't sure whether he was being entirely serious, or whether he was taking the rise out of all of those "seagulls" following his "trawler", expecting a quote). It finished with the chant-style couplet: "Eric Cantona, Eric Cantona, A banana with no 'na', is bana." Revisiting his Cantona "Banargument" of the 1990s, Hegley says: "In terms of Monsieur Cantona: my Dad was a native of France - with a Folies Bergeres dancing mother - and Eric's footballing excellence made me glad to see a Frenchman doing well in my own native land, on behalf of dad and his Mama (Ma-mah)."

With United fans, it was love at first sight. Phil Martin describes Eric's instant impact thus: "Cantona matched the ethos of the club from day one: arrogance, swagger, skill and commitment and raised the bar to a previously unseen level under Fergie."

Here was a player who could make you laugh, he was so *magnifique*. Here was a player who attempted the extraordinary, who showed us glimpses of an earthy heaven. Here was a Rimbaud-quoting, Micky Rourke-loving, part-time painting, catwalk modelling, acting, flicking, tricking, sometimes profoundly daft, sometimes daftly profound, *genius*. Here was a man who embodied everything we all felt about United and more.

He was a catalyst: his signature from Leeds for a paltry £1 million was, without doubt, the most important of Sir Alex's reign. He was a teacher: his influence on youngsters like Giggsy, Beckham and Scholes was crucial in their development. He showed them what benefits they could reap by putting in extra training. How they could polish perfection. He was a leader: there were so many occasions he showed United the way. So many moments he inspired us.

And yet, despite the puffed-out chest and the upturned collar, despite the strutting, off the field this French cockerel was refreshingly free of ego. Fergie loved working with Eric and, when the

Frenchman returned to France to lick his wounds after the Simmonds ban, Sir Alex flew out to plead with Eric not to leave Old Trafford. (Ferguson made allowances for Eric too: ex-Red players often refer to the time the United squad were invited to Manchester town hall for a mayoral reception. Ferguson had instructed the players to turn up suited and booted, and yet Cantona turned up in jeans and a tee shirt. If he'd been anyone else – Lee Sharpe maybe – he'd have been given the full on Fergie-fury, but as it was Eric, nothing was said.) And the inimitable film director Ken Loach, who worked with Cantona on the fantastic *Looking for Eric,* said when interviewed for this book: "We don't usually work with stars, but we made an exception for Eric – and what a star! And a team player too. No hair dryer needed on this job!"

Opposition fans, of course, loathed him. After much arm-twisting, I managed to secure a 'view from the enemy' from the club he left for Old Trafford. When pressed for a comment, Robert Endeacott, who runs the website Dirty Leeds.net, and who has written authoratively on Leeds United FC and football in general, in books such as *Dirty Leeds* (2009), and also, *Disrepute: Revie's England* (2010) offered this back-handed compliment:

"Cantona always got my goat, simply because his sale was as bad as our purchase of Giles and much later, Strachan's move from Manchester United *to* Leeds."

Eric had been loved in Leeds. He brought the 'fantasy' to a team otherwise full of stubborn British grit. They'd beat Manchester United to the last ever First Division championship in 1991-92, and yet, in 1992-93, Howard Wilkinson fell out with the French star the fans used to serenade with "Ooh Aah" and, to the chagrin of those same fans, he soon ended up in the arms of their arch nemesis, Alex Ferguson. The transfer happened by chance. Legend has it that the Leeds United chairman Bill Fotherby called his Manchester United counterpart, Martin Edwards, in order to try and sign the full-back Denis Irwin, who'd previously played for Leeds. Edwards, who, at the time of the call was meeting with Fergie, put his hand over the receiver. Mouthed the name "Irwin". Fergie shook his head. No way. And then, by chance, he mouthed back the name "Cantona". United were desperate to make quality additions to the striking department at the time, as they were struggling for goals in the new Premier League. Eric Cantona, who'd already scored the first ever Premier League hat-trick for Leeds,

243

definitely fitted the bill. But surely Leeds wouldn't sell? Would they?

Both Ferguson and Edwards were surprised by Leeds' enthusiasm for the deal. Howard Wilkinson wanted Eric out of the club and Fotherby wanted to ensure they received a fee for him. £1 million, however, seemed like peanuts. Like paying tuppence ha'penny for a Van Gogh. United snapped their hands off, and the course of history was changed forever.

Eric made his debut as a substitute in a 2-1 win against local rivals Manchester City at Old Trafford on 6th December 1992. His first goal came two weeks later, in a 1-1 draw at Stamford Bridge against Chelsea. But it was his second which offered a glimpse of what was to come from the Frenchman. 3-0 down against Sheffield Wednesday on Boxing Day, Eric was one of the scorers as United improbably pulled it back to 3-3, showing a new indomitable spirit which would serve them well as they plotted their course to a first title in 26 years. United had been eighth when Eric signed. He completely revitalised the club, gave us a new confidence, a new swagger. They eventually went on to win the league by a full 10 points, after a

staggering, Cantona-inspired second half to the
season in which they won seven games on the trot at
the make-or-break time of April (where they'd
stumbled a year previously).

But if Eric was the name on everyone's lips
for the second half of 1992-93, he completely
dominated the *whole* of the next season, 1993-94, in
which United won their first ever double (with
Cantona scoring a brace of penalties against Chelsea
in the FA Cup final). He was the PFA Player of the
Year, but he also showed the first signs of his fabled
red-mist. Of course, we'd heard all about his antics
in France: how he'd thrown boots in the face of a
teammate, how he'd called each and every member
of a France FA disciplinary panel a "sack of s**t",
how he'd thrown a ball at a referee in disgust. But
until he was sent off at Galatasaray as United
crashed out of the Champions League in "Hell", we
hadn't seen him replicate this rage in a Red shirt. To
be fair, in Istanbul, he was provoked. He saw he'd
been wronged, and he set about taking the law into
his own hands. Same thing later that season, when
he saw red twice in a week – first against Swindon,
for a stamp on John Moncur, then, unfortunately,
against Arsenal for, well, not much really. He
received a five-match ban for these indiscretions,

and one of the game he missed was the FA Cup semi-final against Oldham, at Wembley. *Without* Eric, United struggled to find their goal-scoring touch, and only a late *golazo* from Mark Hughes spared United's blushes.

But these disciplinary issues were mere footnotes when compared with what was to come in the 1994-95 season. *That* game at Crystal Palace. *That* sending-off for a flick of the leg against the Palace defender, Richard Shaw. *That* trudge to the tunnel. *That* pause, when he heard some insult from the crowd. *That* mad, bad, dangerous, glorious kung-fu kick over the advertising hoardings and into the crowd, into one Matthew Simmonds. *That* arrest. *That* court case. *That* community service order. *That* United ban. *That* FA ban, which ridiculously trumped the United ban, leaving him out of action until October the following season. *That* press conference afterwards when he muttered, enigmatically into the microphone: "When the seagulls follow the trawler, it's because they think sardines will be thrown into the sea." *Those* wobbly moments when he almost turned his back on English football, on United, on Fergie.

Of course, he scored on his comeback, against Liverpool, in a 2-2 draw. And he celebrated wildly, pole-dancing on a post behind the goal which supported the Old Trafford netting, screaming into the M16 air. But after this incredible return, he struggled for form and fitness. As you would after nearly eight months out. And by Christmas, United trailed Kevin Keegan's Newcastle United by a hefty ten points. It was then, when United were being written off, when *Cantona* was being written off, that King Eric stepped up to the plate, determined to make up for what United had lost in his absence (they'd finished as runners-up in both the Premier League and FA Cup without him.)

In early 1996, United went on a blistering ten game winning run which reigned in Newcastle. During this time, they beat the Geordies at St. James' Park, with a goal from Eric completely against the run of play (Schmeichel had made save after save). Andy Rivers, author of the Newcastle United-inspired *I'm Rivelinho* winces when he recalls this unstoppable United run: "Undoubtedly it was Cantona and Schmeichel who won United the league in '96 when we (Newcastle) should have. Manchester United weren't playing that well but went on a run where Schmeichel would save everything and

Cantona would score a goal against the run of play to get United a 1-0 win. Every week. And when United did exactly that at St. James' Park after Newcastle had absolutely murdered United, that was the moment the title started to slip away – probably never to come back in my lifetime...cheers Eric you t**t!"

But the most famous 1-0 win of 1996 came in the FA Cup final, against Liverpool. With Steve Bruce absent through injury, Eric wore the captain's armband and put in the complete skipper's performance throughout. And in the 87th minute, he scored the winner, sliding an impossible, improbable shot through a forest of Scouse legs, sparking mass jubilation amongst the travelling Reds.

Cantona's last trophy came in 1996-97, as United retained the Premier League title (Cantona's fourth championship in five years at United – what would have happened had he not launched himself into the crowd at Palace?) He announced his retirement from football at just 30. He'd been like a blazing comet which had burned brightly in our skies for a few years. But, if Reds squint a little, they can still see the trail of light he left behind.

He's still the most popular United player of the Ferguson era. He's still bar-none, the number one selling shirt from T-shirts United. He's still a hero.

It was John Lennon (again) who said this: "My role in society, or any artist's or poet's role, is to try and express what we all feel. Not to tell people how to feel. Not as a preacher, not as a leader, but as a reflection of us all." Substitute Cantona for Lennon and you're on the right path. Cantona was a reflection of us all, in the most flattering of mirrors.

Verdict: Phil Bedford at T-Shirts United summed up the thoughts of many United fans when I asked him for his thoughts on 'Team Fergie'. He suggested the ideal line-up would include "Peter Schmeichel in goal, with five Bryan Robsons and five Eric Cantonas (with Ole Gunnar Solksjaer as sub)."

His five Cantonas comment recalls one of the many, many United songs dedicated to King Eric, in this case *The 12 Days of Christmas* (with five Cantonas replacing the "five go-old rings", *etcetera*

249

etcetera). There are others. To the tune of *Lily the Pink:* "We'll drink-a-drink-a-drink to Eric the king, the king, the king; He's the leader of our football team. He's the greatest centre forward, that the world has ever seen." To the tune of *La Marseillaise:* "Ooh Aah Cantona", *ad infinitum.*

Eric Cantona was like The Stone Roses, The Happy Mondays, James Dean, Marlon Brando, Vincent Cassel, Denis Law, Zinedine Zidane, and Han Solo all rolled into one. Effortlessly cool, fantastically talented, angry, and soulful. Those who don't get Cantona, don't get United, don't get *life.*

He *has to* make the cut.

Simply *magnifique.*

11 - Striker

The night United claimed their thirteenth Premier League title, on 22nd April 2013 found Sir Alex Ferguson in something of a reflective mood. Of course, we all know now that he'd decided to retire. And as well as celebrating the reclamation of the title from "noisy neighbours" Manchester City, the mammoth points haul of the current side saw him giving serious consideration as to whether the 2012-13 incarnation of the Reds was the best he'd ever seen at the club. Certainly the strikers had staked a claim. After United had lost out on the previous season's championship on goal difference, Fergie had sworn this would never happen again.

And so he went out and bought the current Premier League top scorer, Robin Van Persie, from rivals Arsenal.

Fergie has always loved his strikers (perhaps because he used to be one). And he admitted we've witnessed some special ones during his tenure: "I've had some great strikers, maybe 10 great strikers." In the previous entry, we considered the candidates for the role of 'deep-lying' striker; the 'number 10'; the 'Cantona role'. Now we'll consider the final place in 'Team Fergie': the number 9. And yet again, we face a tough choice:

Robin Van Persie

The Manchester Evening News (MEN) has always given rather, ahem, favourable marks out of ten for United and City players in its match reports. There was a spell in the early 1990s when many Reds genuinely believed Mike Phelan was called 'Phelan 8' because of the sheer number of consecutive 8's handed out to a player whose form at the time was, at best, acceptable. Denis Irwin *always* got an 8 too, unless he scored. Then he'd get a 9. It didn't give much wiggle-room in the event of a truly magnificent performance of the Roy-Keane-in-Turin or Eric-Cantona-at-any-time-in-1996 mould. A brace pretty much guaranteed a player a 10.

But perhaps Manchester's local paper can be forgiven for their generosity. After all, it was those same players they were grading that they'd have to go to on the following Tuesday, looking for a quote before the match on Wednesday. And why would a player want to help out a journalist if they'd just been given a 3? There was probably another consideration for the *MEN* writers. They were likely bricking themselves that if they did give a player a below-par grading, then one Sir Alex Ferguson was very likely to find them out – he was renowned for reading everything – and give them the old hairdryer treatment.

Still, in the history of *MEN* reporting, it's pretty certain that no player has ever scored as highly in the match ratings as Robin Van Persie, after his hat-trick performance in the championship-clinching game against Aston Villa at Old Trafford on 22nd April 2013. For that night, Robin scored an incredible 20/10.

20 was, of course, the number on everyone's lips. Van Persie, upon signing for the club from Arsenal, was offered his choice of squad numbers. He'd opted for the number 20. He knew the symbolism of the number: 2012-13 was – all being well – going to be the season United claimed their 20th league championship. It was also the shirt

number of one of the greatest Red heroes of the Ferguson era: Ole Gunnar Solksjaer.

They broke the mould when they made Robin Van Persie. The archetypal Rolls Royce of a player, he is sleek, quick, and devastating.

United broke the mould when they *signed* Van Persie. Sure he was the Premier League top scorer the precious season, and sure he was playing by far the best football of his career, but he was 29 years old, and famously injury-prone (there is a sense that the Dutchman plays at such a highly-tuned level, even the slightest niggle can consign him to the sidelines). And, during previous summer transfer windows, Fergie had shown a marked reluctance to take a gamble on anyone older than, say, twenty-six. And indeed, this had become a club policy: Dimitar Berbatov was supposed to be the last *over-* twenty-six year old we'd ever sign. What's more, Sir Alex constantly harped on that there was no "value in the market".

But there were extenuating circumstances. At the bitter end of the 2011-12 season, Manchester City had beaten United to the title on goal difference. And so, when Van Persie announced on his own website that he'd be leaving Arsenal,

Ferguson just knew he had to go in for him. The need to sign him was increased after City began to talk up their interest in the player. Eventually, Robin went Red, and City, in the form of their manager, Roberto Mancini, spent seemingly the whole of the 2012-13 season bemoaning the fact Van Persie hadn't signed for them.

He hadn't. Because the "little boy inside him" had told him United were the team he should choose. And how history has proved him right: RVP the MVP of the 2012-13 season.

But it's a little known fact that, if it wasn't for the little boy inside Robin, he might have joined the Old Trafford club much earlier. In 2001, Fergie dispatched chief scout Jim Ryan on a spying mission to Holland, only for Robin to see red. Ryan's report back to Sir Alex was glowing in its praise for RVP, but it also drew the manager's attention to his "immaturity".

Still, he got here in the end, after a detour - nine years at Arsenal, where he won just one FA Cup.

In another 'Team Fergie' profile, we discussed how Mark Hughes was not necessarily a

255

great goal-scorer, but he was a scorer of great goals. Robin Van Persie is a great goal-scorer of great goals. He scored a blockbuster against Fulham (on his Old Trafford debut), and a wonderful header against Southampton. His goals helped United come from behind in eight league games at the start of the season. And his run of 12 goals in 14 matches between November and February allowed United to make great strides in the title race and effectively leave City for dust by mid-February. His best goal, however, came in the coronation game against Aston Villa at Old Trafford. In the 14th minute, he volleyed a long Wayne Rooney pass, which came at him over his shoulder, past Brad Guzan before the American even had time to blink. Fergie described the goal as "the goal of the century", though perhaps the celebrations had gotten to his head at this point.

Most importantly though, he had a very good record against our Premier League rivals. He scored an injury time free-kick winner at the Etihad to beat Manchester City 3-2 (after City had come back from 2-0 down). He scored at Stamford Bridge against Chelsea. He scored against Arsenal home and away. He scored against Liverpool home and away.

Increasingly, it seemed that Robin Van Persie had a new middle name: he'd become Robin 'The Difference' Van Persie. As far back as Boxing Day, Ferguson was in full agreement. In his programme notes for the game against Newcastle, Sir Alex wrote that he had "no hesitation saying he (RVP) has made a vital difference…" Fans knew it too. Van Persie's name was now the one sung above all the others. ("Oh Robin Van Persie" to the tune of The White Stripes' 'Seven Nation Army'.)

The only slight negative of RVP's first season at United came in the Champions League. He fluffed a couple of half-chances at the Bernabeu against Real Madrid which could have secured United a very decent first leg lead.

However, this would only be a minor quibble because the number one priority for Van Persie, his United teammates, Fergie, and especially the fans, was wrestling that Premier League crown back from the "noisy neighbours" across the city. Stopping us from having to watch *that* Sergio Aguero goal on every Sky Sports broadcast and at the end of the *Match of the Day* trail on a weekly basis. Allowing us to celebrate again.

And how.

257

Ruud Van Nistelrooy

But RVP is far from our only Dutch MVP. Back in the early noughties, we had the original Red Van Man. According to Neil Custis, Ruud Van Nistelrooy was "the ultimate predator", Red in tooth and claw. He was the *apex* predator in the Premier League during his United years. He was top of the food chain. He had the crocodilian cunning of a Wayne Rooney and the strength of a tiger. He could swoop like an eagle and had the pace - over short distances – of a cheetah. And it didn't matter if the rest of his ecosystem – his team – was unhealthy, or underperforming. No: when Ruud was on song, when he *purred,* then fans could be sure of a United win.

Van Nistelrooy was lethal. He was a snarlingly efficient killer of chances with both feet. Good in the air, too. He came alive in the opposition's penalty box like a panther on the prowl. And though he 'only' won one Premier League title with United, as well as an FA Cup and a League Cup, he tore into opponents domestically and abroad. "He just knew where to be and when to put that ball away," says Neil Custis. Indeed, Ruud had a tremendous goal-scoring record: he scored 150 goals in 219 games in all competitions for the Reds (and out of those 150, there were probably two from outside the box.)

Scott The Red, editor of the excellent TheRepublikOfMancunia.com website, is an unabashed admirer of Van Nistelrooy: "Ruud may not be the most decorated striker at United but his goal-scoring record was incredible. Also, he was a bit of a nasty c**t and I like players who have an edge to them. He was a key figure in those battles with Arsenal that were so enjoyable over the years."

Ah, that rivalry with Arsenal. There's not been one like it in the Ferguson era. Sure we've had Chelsea, who, especially under Mourinho provided ultra-stiff competition, but there was a sense there was something *manufactured* about them. Same with Manchester City now. And then there's Liverpool… But against Liverpool it's just *too* painful to lose. There is *too much* hatred involved… Against Arsenal the teams were both built properly, by proper managers. They contained proper players. Men. The two teams were very well-matched. They were equally driven to win, and equally angry when they lost. There were some titanic battles which stirred

259

the blood. And, alongside Keane and Vieira, two of the major players were Ruud Van Nistelrooy and his nemesis, Martin Keown. The pair of them kept up a running battle over a whole series of matches which was reminiscent of the McClair-Winterburn rivalry of Ferguson days of yore. There was always that bite, that edge in the games. You couldn't take your eye off the ball, but often if you did, you saw there was something else going on, something tasty.

It was a true battle to be the apex predator, the alpha team in the land. It was wonderful to watch. The United faithful loved Van Nistelrooy with a Red-blooded passion they hadn't shown for that other arch-predator Andy Cole, or for Brian McClair for that matter. He was so obviously world class, so obviously brilliant at what he did, and he was also so obviously driven. We sung, to the tune of *Karma Chameleon:* "Ruudy, Ruudy, Ruudy, Ruudy, Ruudy, Van Nistelrooy. Van Nistelrooy, Van Nistelrooy." Or, during one season, in a chant reminiscent of the "drums from the deep" music in *Lord of the Rings,* a guttural grunt of "Ruud… Ruud… Ruud." He was our not-so-secret weapon, our stealth missile, and more often than not, he hit the target.

RVN has always scored goals. In his early career he played little over 30 games for Den Bosch, in the Dutch second division, but his record convinced Heerenveen to shell out for him. And then, after only one season at the Friesland club, Dutch giants PSV Eindhoven snapped him up. His transfer was a then-record between two Dutch clubs. And it was at PSV that Ruud began to sharpen his claws. He hunted down virtually a goal a game in his first season and had a similar record in the next.

And it was in this second season that Van Nistelrooy was first spotted by United 'scouts'. Darren Ferguson, Sir Alex's son who'd played 27 games for United under his father's tutelage, was on trial with Van Nistelrooy's former club Heerenveen. He spotted Ruud and called his Fergie Snr. Immediately, begging him to sign the PSV forward. Sir Alex gave in to his son's pleadings and sent out a team of 'proper' scouts to watch Ruud and, within days, a United deal – rumoured to be worth £18.5 million - was on the table. A press conference was called to announce the new signing, only, when the journalists turned up, it was instantly apparent that the mood in the room wasn't the kind they'd have expected. It seemed too gloomy for the announcement of a big-money new-signing. And it was then United announced that the signing had been put 'on hold'. Apparently there were concerns over Ruud's knee. And such concerns weren't without warrant: less than a week later, Van Nistelrooy ruptured his cruciate ligament in training.

Some players don't come back from injuries like that.

Ruud did though. Almost a year later, he proved himself in a United medical, and signed for the Reds for £19 million. He scored 23 league goals in his first season for the Reds and in the following season, improved on that tally by netting 25. He also made the score-sheet in the FA Cup, with two in the final against Millwall, to win the trophy.

Ruud won the Sir Matt Busby Award for the United player of the year in 2001-02, and 2002-03, becoming only the second player – after Roy Keane – to win the award in consecutive seasons (Cristiano Ronaldo also went on to achieve this, winning a total of three awards overall, which makes him the only player to achieve this.) Other players who have won the award twice include Brian McClair, Eric Cantona and Wayne Rooney (making this one area in which Van Nistelrooy has actually out-achieved Ryan

Giggs, the holder of seemingly every other United-based record).

In 2004-05, however, injuries came back to haunt the Dutchman. He missed large chunks of the season due to knee problems, but still managed a remarkable eight goals in the Champions League. In the process, he beat Denis Law's European goal-scoring record for United. In 2005-06 though, Van Nistelrooy started the season as though desperate to make up for the time he'd lost in the previous season. He started like the proverbial burning house, scoring in the first four games of the season and everything looked set for the Dutchman's best year yet in a United shirt. The rest of the team had improved around him by this time and now, with Wayne Rooney and Cristiano blazing a trail for the Reds, the goal-scoring responsibilities didn't only fall to Ruud. However, this was the moment it all went wrong for Ruud at United. A training ground fight with Ronaldo sparked his exclusion from the squad – he missed the League Cup final win against Wigan and was benched for a further seven Premier League games as United went into the business end of the season. Two years previously, the fight would have seen *Ronaldo* out of the squad. Back then, Ruud had been our undoubted number one player. But now, in

2006, in Ronaldo and Rooney Ferguson could see United's future.

United cashed in on Van Nistelrooy in the close-season. He signed with Real Madrid for a similar fee to the one United had paid PSV Eindhoven for his services five years previously. At Madrid, he finished the *La Liga* top scorer in his first season (winning the *Pichichi)* and equaled and broke goal-scoring records along the way. He eventually retired in May 2012, after (rather toothless) post-Madrid spells at Hamburg and Malaga. But in his prime, the Ruud Boy was perhaps the sharpest forward United fans have ever seen at Old Trafford.

Andy Cole

As you'll have seen from the cover of this book, my name is Andrew. But I'm not bothered if you call me Andy. I write fiction too, and for that, I'm known as AJ. In fact, you can call me what you want as long as you buy, and enjoy the books. This isn't the case for

Andy 'Andrew' Cole. No: 'Goal King Cole' came over all kinds of surly when you called him Andy, especially towards the latter stages of his career. I'm not sure why he felt this way. But then again, Coley often seemed to get a little 'antsy' about the most trivial of things – witness his extended silence, when he and Teddy Sheringham refused to speak to each other for *years* after one mis-placed pass in a game.

So you'd have thought Andy Cole might not have time for the fripperies and foolishness of the ever-smiling Dwight Yorke. You'd have thought he'd have returned that trademark Yorkie grin with a sneer. But that wasn't what happened. The unlikely duo were to strike a partnership deal which saw both find the best form of their careers during a devastating two year spell at United. The understanding they had bordered on the telepathic. You often wondered whether they might take a turn as street magicians when their football careers were done and dusted.

Yeah, Coley and Yorke clicked, and in a big way. They brought out the best in each other, and in the United team. When they were good, they were very, very good. And when they were great, they won a treble.

265

But before that, before Yorke arrived, the Nottingham-born Cole had a whole other career at Old Trafford. United paid a British record transfer fee of £7 million to Newcastle United for the star in January 1995. Newcastle supporters – many of whom had recently had Coley tattoos inked on their bodies following his sparkling form in the Premier League – were so enamoured with the decision to sell their number 9 that manager Kevin Keegan had to come out of some back exit at St. James' Park in order to – somewhat sheepishly – explain his decision. And Cole was to enjoy a marvellous first season for the Reds. To a point. He scored an excellent 12 goals in 18 games in the remainder of the season (including 5 in a 9-0 drubbing of Ipswich Town), but ultimately his 1994-95 will be more remembered for his misses.

On 14 May 1995 United were away at West Ham – that perennial graveyard of Red dreams – knowing that if they won, they'd secure the Premier League title. Late on, United launched into a customary all-out assault on the opposition box in the desperate search for a winner. There was a sense that a goal was coming. And United created two very presentable chances during a frenetic last ten minutes, both of which fell to Cole. Both of which

Cole spurned. The second chance in particular was galling for fans. Cole, confronted by an onrushing Ludek Miklosko, simply had to lift the ball over the West Ham 'keeper to win the match. But he chose wrong. Hit it low, and Miklosko saved. United drew and Blackburn Rovers were the champions.

It was this game more than any other which gave rise to the narrative in which Cole needed "at least five chances to score". Glenn Hoddle, when he was England manager, was to jump on this as an excuse for not picking Cole even when Andy (Andrew) was on top form for United. Even those Newcastle fans who'd so loved him when he played in the north east, now made out they'd never been convinced by the number 9. Andy Rivers, author of the Newcastle United-inspired *I'm Rivelinho,* says: "Newcastle made Cole, Kevin Keegan took him from obscurity (from Bristol City), put Peter Beardsley next to him to ensure he got plenty of chances per game (which he needed as he missed loads) and he still left. That being said, it was the correct decision to sell him to Manchester United at the time, as he was being found out in the Newcastle team and needed a new challenge. He seemed to delight in scoring past us though (and he did it often the t**t!) and I could never understand why really.

267

Like I say, if it wasn't for Newcastle, he would have finished his career in the lower divisions as a prolific Steve Bull-type that no big club would take a chance on."

So there were strong suspicions that Andrew Cole was something of a chancer. That he was lucky to be in the right place at the right time. There were some who said Cole's ill-advised 'pop career', which was based on the ironically titled 'Outstanding' - which reached about number 67 in the charts – was an indication that though he thought he was great, not many other people agreed.

It seemed Eric Cantona had 'found Cole out'. When partnered with Cole in the former Newcastle man's first season, Eric often couldn't disguise his disgust at Cole's misplaced passes, his 'wrong wavelength', his erratic finishing. But Cole was to put all this to one side as his goal won the FA Cup semi-final against Chelsea, and he also scored one of the three which beat Middlesbrough to secure the Premier League title. 1996-97 followed much the same script, with Cole largely inconsistent. He was fantastic as United thrashed Porto at Old Trafford in the Champions League, and as he scored at Anfield to win another title, but still, the emergence of

Solksjaer was increasingly putting his place in the starting line-up in some doubt.

And Cole was to be placed on even shakier ground at the start of 1998-99 when *another* striker arrived. This time it was to be Dwight Yorke from Aston Villa, and indeed, there was a chance Cole might have gone the other way as a make-weight. Certainly that was what the Villa manager John Gregory pressed for. But Cole stayed, and forged a wonderful relationship – both on and off the field - with the man who might have been his replacement. Between them, they scored 53 goals that season, and at times they were simply unplayable. Cole scored the goal that secured United the first part of the treble: the winner in a Premier League game against Spurs at Old Trafford. He also scored the winner in Turin, in the 'Keane' semi-final, when United came from 2-0 down to beat Juventus 3-2 on aggregate.

Two more titles were to follow, in 1999-2000 and 2000-01. But the Cole and Yorke tandem never hit the same heights as they'd done in their first, honeymoon year. Eventually, the arrival of the arch-predator Ruud Van Nistelrooy put paid to Cole's first-team chances, as did a Fergie re-think, which saw United line up as a defensive 4-5-1 (or an

269

attacking 4-3-3) in the big domestic and European games. Cole eventually moved on, to Blackburn, for £8 million. (After that, he became something of a journeyman, turning out for Fulham, Manchester City, Portsmouth, Birmingham City, Sunderland, Burnley, and his home town club, Nottingham Forest).

Andy Cole played a total of 275 matches for the Reds, scoring 121 goals. He won five Premier League titles, one Champions League, and two FA Cups for United.

Ole Gunnar Solksjaer

In Norse mythology, Loki was something of a trickster god. He loved nothing more than creating chaos, upsetting the apple-cart, confounding expectations. And in Ole Gunnar Solksjaer, United's Norwegian striker, we had our very own Loki. He was the trickster who turned lost causes on their head; the bringer of chaos to terraces across Europe

270

as he rescued games for the Reds, as he brought us back from the dead, and secured us ultimate glory. He was the original

'Baby-faced' assassin, with his cherubic looks, his tight curls, his childish grin. And his killer instinct.

Mention the name Ole Gunnar Solksjaer to any Red, and a mischievous smile will tickle the corners of their mouth. That'll be them, remembering exactly where they were - whether they were in the Nou Camp, or the Trafford pub, or their own front room – when Ole scored *that* goal to win the Champions League, and the treble, for Manchester United, causing wide-spread chaos. The gods had already spoken in that match. The winner was decided. Bayern Munich were *supposed* to triumph, by a goal to nil. Ribbons in Munich's colours had already been draped on the trophy. Players were already thinking about how they'd celebrate. And then Ole (and Teddy) popped up with two trickster goals, and suddenly chaos was invoked.

The hairs on the back of the neck will stand on end. Reds in the stadium that night will remember a feeling of such utterly unexpected joy

271

that it was as though the streams had been crossed in *Ghostbusters.* Those watching in pubs, or at home, will recall *that* Clive Tyldesley commentary (perhaps the most famous commentary in the history of Manchester United): "And Solksjaer has *won* it for Manchester United." And: "Manchester United have reached the promised land."

Phil Martin talks of how "Ole will always have *that* instinctive toe poke into the top corner in the Champions League final, and the fact he sent us to a level of euphoric celebration that no English club has ever matched." Grown men were crying (and not in a Newcastle way). Families reunited. Students sacrificed whole years of their lives by going out celebrating instead of staying in and preparing for their final exams the next day. People drank and shouted and laughed and danced and decided that if football ended that evening, if we could never see United again, then it would still have been worth it just to see Ole's goal. Sir Alex swore on live TV. Solksjaer slid on his knees (and probably set in motion the knee-problems which would plague his latter years at the club).

Like I said, Ole brought chaos.

The following day, fans flocked to Manchester to see the team on an open-top bus ride around the city. Fans skived off work to hang off lampposts, traffic lights and out of windows just to catch a glimpse of our returning heroes. The bus's number was 2-1, recognising the score in the final. And just above that, you could see Dwight Yorke, Andy Cole, and Teddy Sheringham clutching the big three trophies the club had won. Further back, Ole Gunnar looked a little sheepish, as though he hadn't been aware of just how much chaos he'd wrought.

And his Champions League goal isn't the only one which will make it into the United hall of fame. Ole's goal-scoring feats for United were superlative. There was his winner, deep, deep into stoppage time against Liverpool in the FA Cup – also in 1999 – which *again* brought the Reds back from the dead. United had been 1-0 down with 5 minutes to go, until Yorke, and then Ole, sparked chaos. There was his truly amazing substitute's display against Nottingham Forest at the City Ground: when he entered the field of play, United were 4-1 up with a half-hour to play. Ole struck *four* times when he came on, taking United's tally to a bullish 8 (*eight*) -1.

273

Ole was a hero. Not a *cult* hero; he was universally liked: he is the number two selling shirt from T-shirts United, behind only King Eric. There is *still* a banner proclaiming "*20 Le*gend" in the Stretford End. And United fans *still sing* about him nearly every week. Over his United years, there were many variations on the song, but in essence, they were about the same thing: his bringing of chaos. And so it was "Who put the ball in the German's/ Scouser's/ *add your own* net? Ole Gunnar Solksjaer." And, to the tune of 'You are my Sunshine': "You are my Solksjaer, my Ole Solksjaer, you make me happy, when skies are grey. And Alan Shearer was f**king dearer, oh please don't take my Solksjaer away." Mums loved him, die-hard home and away fans loved him, old-timers loved him. Ole brought a trickster gleam to the eye of anyone you asked about him.

It wasn't all about the goals though. We loved Ole because he so clearly loved the club. Because he'd give his all for it: sacrifice himself if he had to. Another famous Ole moment is the one against Newcastle in 1998. The match was tied at 1-1, however Rob Lee, the Magpies' midfielder was suddenly clear on goal. Ole was to run the length of the field in order to undertake a rugby tackle on Lee, receiving the most obvious red card of the season for his trouble, but the important thing – to him, and to fans – was the fact he saved the point for United. He was given a standing ovation as he stalked off the field.

So it wasn't just about the bald stats and the goals. Solksjaer played a total of 336 games for the Reds, including substitute appearances – of which there were many. He scored 126 goals. But that is not even a *quarter* of the story of the impact he had. He won six Premier League titles, one Champions League, and two FA Cups, but those bare statistics do not even scratch the surface when it comes to analyzing his place as a true Red legend.

Like I said, Ole was the bringer of chaos. He joined United from Molde (where he is now a successful manager) in 1996, for a fee of £1.5 million. United had been after Alan Shearer at the time, but missed out – Shearer was "f**king dearer". And it was not expected he would trouble the first-team for at least a couple of seasons. For a start Cantona and Cole were above him in the striking pecking-order. But Ole had other ideas. The number 20 was surprisingly given a place on the bench for United's first game of the 1996-97 season against

Blackburn and, when he scored as a substitute within five minutes of taking the field, he showed us the template which would serve him for the rest of a United career in which his *team* achievements far outshone those of, for example, Alan Shearer.

Not many players enjoy being dubbed a 'super-sub'. In 2012-13, after a series of goals scored when coming off the bench, the Manchester City player Edin Dzeko said that the last thing in the world he wanted to be known as was a 'super-sub'. No, he wanted to be a starter, the number one. Ole, however, didn't seem to mind. His time on the bench gave him the time to analyse matches before he entered the fray. He spotted gaps, defensive weaknesses, and, when he took the field, he ruthlessly exploited them. This skill, this football-brain, is now one of the reasons Ole is such a highly regarded manager.

There was one last moment of chaos for Ole. *That* knee which he'd slid on after scoring *that* goal in Barcelona, had put paid to practically two full seasons of his United career. There was some doubt over whether he'd ever come back for the Reds. But somehow, against all the odds, he dragged himself back to fitness and made a first-team return in 2006.

Talking of his first goal on the comeback-trail, Sir Alex said: "it was a great moment for Ole, United fans everywhere, the players and the staff". Because the goal meant something to everyone. And indeed, it sparked something of an Ole revival. Fans celebrated that goal – a routine third in an easy win – as though it was the Nou Camp all over again. And after his torrid injury-years Ole scored a number of important goals, including an injury-time goal against Aston Villa in the FA Cup in January 2007. But further complications with his knee eventually curtailed his career. His final game for the Reds was an appearance in the FA Cup final defeat against Chelsea.

By hook or by crook, Ole will be last in his book. Though he was largely a substitute, though he wasn't world class like a Van Nistelrooy or a Van Persie, though he wasn't as skilful as a Yorke or as magnificent as a Cantona, by dint of the pure chaos he set in motion, Ole Gunnar Solksjaer *should* have the final word.

After all, that's what he had throughout his career at the Reds.

Verdict: It would be impossible to choose Andy Cole without his 'telepathic twin' Dwight Yorke, and, as I've not selected Yorkie for 'Team Fergie', then I'm afraid there's no dice for Cole. And though Robin Van Persie has had a fairytale first season for the Reds, that's all it has been. A first season. In time, he'll go on to cement his place in the side, but for now, the achievements of Solksjaer and Van Nistelrooy outweigh those of the Red Robin. The love and affection the fans still have for Ole and Ruud also plays a crucial factor in my decision.

And this is a decision I haven't taken lightly, but sorry, Ole, you're not in the x11. Then again, you were always devastating as a super-sub and maybe you're only on the bench for the chaos you can bring when you come on, with twenty minutes remaining.

And so it falls to Ruud Van Nistelrooy to take the final place in 'Team Fergie'. You can take a look at the team in full, overleaf.

Fergie's Finest: Sir Alex Ferguson's Greatest Manchester United x11

Goalkeeper
Peter Schmeichel

Right-Back	**Centre-Half**	**Centre-Half**	**Full-Back**
Gary Neville	Jaap Stam	Rio Ferdinand	Patrice Evra

Right-Wing	**Central-Midfield**	**Central-Midfield**	**Left-Wing**
C. Ronaldo	Roy Keane	Paul Scholes	Ryan Giggs

Striker	**Striker**
Eric Cantona	Ruud Van Nistelrooy

Super-Subs: Edwin Van Der Sar (GK), Nemanja Vidic (CB), Denis Irwin (LB), David Beckham (RW), Bryan Robson (CM), Ole Gunnar Solksjaer (ST), Wayne Rooney (ST), Robin Van Persie (ST)

279

Manager: Sir Alex Ferguson

Acknowledgements & Thanks

It's been real hard work writing this book and generally talking about football, and United, with a whole range of folk. It's not my favourite thing in the world recalling famous United wins, and goals, and the players I've loved. I don't like interviewing stars like Norman Whiteside and Ken Loach. Not a bit of it.

It's not what I would have been doing anyway, even had I not been writing a book. (And if you've ever spent any time round my house, or with me in the pub, you'll know that's bulls**t. But I have to make this book-writing lark sound like hard yacker, otherwise everyone'll be at it.)

Anyway, on a serious note, I'd like to thank everyone who has 'stuck their oar in', either with a key fact, or an opinion, or a view on a player I 'just can't leave out'. At the risk of this sounding like some kind of Oscar acceptance speech, I've put together a list (below) of the key contributors, a brief bibliography and further reading list, and a few miscellaneous (and thoroughly random) stats.

I've had some great quotes, and I've also had lots of assistance with the factual stuff (the players' prodigious medal hauls for one) but I'd like to stress that any mistakes made are mine   and mine alone. *Mea culpa.*

281

Key Contributors

- Norman Whiteside, red hero and all-round good bloke: www.**normanwhiteside**.com/

- Ken Loach, Director of two fantastic films involving football: *Looking for Eric,* and *Kes* (as well as many others not involving football, including *The Angel's Share* and *The Wind that Shakes the Barley*)

- Neil Custis, Football Writer for The Sun newspaper, covering Manchester United and Manchester City.

- Scott the Red, editor of the excellent Republik of Mancunia website: http://therepublikofmancunia.com/

- Ethel Sleith, Branch Secretary, Manchester United Supporters' Club, South Africa

- John Hegley, one of the country's most innovative comic poets, regularly sells out at the Edinburgh Festival, and writes great stuff about King Eric: http://www.johnhegley.co.uk/

- Phil Martin, Manchester-based author and match-goer since 1985. Visit his website here: http://philmartinbooks.co.uk/ Or read his fantastic poetry (about Lou Macari's chip shop

282

amongst other things) here:
http://philmartinauthor.blogspot.co.uk/

- Dr. R.G. Kirby, author of the Manchester history book *The Voice of the People,* and my dad… The man to blame for my United obsession.

- Phil Bedford, at T-Shirts United:
  http://www.redmolotov.com/

- Hugh Evans, from Soccer Starz, the manufacturers of football figurines:
  http://www.soccerstarz.com/index.php#

- David Pearson, Deputy Director, National Football Museum:
  http://www.nationalfootballmuseum.com/

- Daniel Pearce, Arsenal Season Ticket Holder.

- Leigh Fairhurst, Manchester City fan and match-goer (and my sister's husband)

- Jenny Fairhurst, Manchester United season-ticket holder for almost as long as me, and my sister.

- Andy Rivers, author of the Newcastle United-inspired *I'm Rivelinho.* Visit his website here:
  http://andyrivers.co.uk

- Robert Endeacott, author of various Leeds United, and England books: http://www.dirtyleeds.net/

Bibliography

- Barclay, Patrick, *Football – Bloody Hell! The Biography of Alex Ferguson,* Yellow Jersey Press, 2010
- Blatt, David, *Manchester United Ruined My Wife,* Know the Score Books, 2008
- Crick, Michael, *The Boss: The Many Sides of Alex Ferguson,* Simon and Schuster, 2002
- Ferguson, Alex, *Alex Ferguson: Managing My Life,* Hodder and Stoughton, 1999
- Kurt, Richard, *United! Despatches from Old Trafford,* Mainstream Publishing, 1999
- Matheson, Stuart, "How the Champions Rated", in *Manchester Evening News,* Wednesday 24 April 2013
- Robson, James, "Simply the best!", *Manchester Evening News,* Wednesday 24 April 2013
- Sharpe, Lee, *My Idea of Fun,* Orion, 2005
- Stam, Jaap, *Head to Head,* Willow, August 2001.

- South, Craig (Producer), A Paul Doherty International Production, *Manchester United: Alex Ferguson's Ultimate United,* 1997
- Wells, Steven, "Rooney: a snap judgement", in *The Guardian,* Monday 30 December 2002

Other Quotations

I've also taken the liberty of paraphrasing four of my favourite poems: Percy Bysshe Shelley's *Ozymandias,* Rudyard Kipling's *If,* WH Auden's *Stop all the clocks,* and Dylan Thomas's *Do not go gentle into that good night.* Look them up and have a read. Fantastic. Thanks also to John Winston Lennon for saying some excellent stuff about Jesus.

Miscellaneous Stats

Finally, for those amongst you hungry to chow down on a few stats (and no, Luis Suarez, I'm not inviting you to bite), here's the chart of the top ten best-selling United figures between 1995 and 2008 from Corinthian. (Strangely there is no room for Ruud van Nistelrooy or Ronaldo, though there is in 'Team Fergie'.)

1. Eric Cantona
2. Ryan Giggs
3. David Beckham
4. Jaap Stam
5. Roy Keane
6. Peter Schmeichel
7. Wayne Rooney
8. Paul Scholes
9. Rio Ferdinand
10. Juan Sebastian Veron

About the Author

Andrew J Kirby's sports writing has featured in BBC
Sport magazine, on the Radio Five Live website, and in
Home Defence UK magazine, where he writes about
'non-league football hooligans'. He spent a season writing
for the Professional Footballers' Association on their
website Give Me Football. He has held a Manchester
United season ticket for the entirety of the Sir Alex
Ferguson reign at Old Trafford, and regularly follows the
Reds across Europe and beyond.

He also writes award-winning crime/ noir fiction
as AJ Kirby, and has five published novels under his belt
(Sharkways, 2012; Paint this Town Red, which was
shortlisted for the Guardian's Not the Booker Prize 2012;
Perfect World, 2011; Bully, which charted as an Amazon

genre number 1 in 2009; The Magpie Trap, 2008), as well as two collections of short stories (The Art of Ventriloquism, a collection of crime shorts, which was released August 2012, and Mix Tape 2010), three novellas (The Haunting of Annie Nicol, 2012; The Black Book, 2011; Call of the Sea, 2010), and over fifty published short stories, which can be found widely in print anthologies, magazines and journals and across the web in zines, writing sites and more. His short fiction has won numerous awards at UK literary festivals.

He also reviews fiction for The New York Journal of Books.

To find out more, check out Andrew's author website here: www.andykirbythewriter.20m.com, or his blog, here: http://paintthistownred.wordpress.com

Printed in Great Britain
by Amazon